THE NATURE OF THE BEAST

Are animals moral?

THE NATURE OF THE BEAST

Are animals moral?

Stephen R. L. Clark

Oxford   New York
OXFORD UNIVERSITY PRESS
1984

Oxford University Press, Walton Street, Oxford OX2 6DP

London Glasgow New York Toronto
Delhi Bombay Calcutta Madras Karachi
Kuala Lumpur Singapore Hong Kong Tokyo
Nairobi Dar es Salaam Cape Town
Melbourne Auckland

and associated companies in
Beirut Berlin Ibadan Mexico City Nicosia

Oxford is a trade mark of Oxford University Press

© Stephen R. L. Clark 1982

First published 1982 by Oxford University Press
First issued as an Oxford University Press paperback 1984

British Library Cataloguing in Publication Data

Clark, Stephen R. L.
The nature of the beast - (Oxford paperbacks)
1. Ethics 2. Animal behaviour
I. Title
170 BJ1031

ISBN 0-19-283041-4

Library of Congress Cataloging in Publication Data

Clark, Stephen R. L.
The nature of the beast, are animals moral?
(Oxford paperbacks)
Bibliography: p.
Includes index.
1. Ethics. 2. Psychology, Comparative.
3. Animals, Habits and behavior of. I. Title.
(BJ1031.C5 1984) 170 83-23658

ISBN 0-19-283041-4 (pbk.)

Keyed by Bernadette Mohan
on a Rank Xerox 850 word-processor
and reproduced photolithographically
direct from the print-out
Printed in Great Britain by
The Guernsey Press Co. Ltd
Guernsey, Channel Islands

PREFACE

Past ages have had their bestiaries and fables, marvels and moral stories. Moralists have employed what they knew or imagined of our non-human kindred to excite scorn or simple piety: how vilely animals behave, or, with what natural morality! Our own age has studied the problem in greater depth and with greater care: we too have brought our presuppositions to the task, though there have been enough scholars, enough funds, enough imagination to correct at least our most egregious errors of observation and theory. But we still find our visions of wickedness among the beasts: hardly a month goes by without a judge or journalist proclaiming that someone has 'become an animal' or 'lives like an animal'. At the same time, we half hope to find that 'other animals' can live in peace and friendship, that our own sad history is an aberration, that we can learn from the beasts. What follows is my attempt to come to grips with some of these problems.

I believe that moral philosophers should take account of their colleagues' investigations into animal behaviour and motivation, and the evolutionary explanations of that behaviour. Many of us do: the popular view that philosophers only want to know what English words can mean, and only investigate by introspection, was never wholly fair and is now quite out of date. But scholarly specialization does sometimes keep us from knowing all we should. Accounts of animal life in philosophical textbooks derive too often from the medieval bestiary and its like.

Similarly, ethologists and animal psychologists would benefit from a more carefully philosophical approach. I do not think that the time is yet ripe for a full-scale philosophy of ethology (or of biology): the discipline is too young, too fluid to be trapped. A lot of verbal confusion can be forgiven when invention is thereby encouraged. Nor do working scholars always need to grapple with the methodological puzzles I try to tackle, and perhaps overemphasize. But I do not think any harm is done by pointing out what ethologists really ought not to say, what shifts and ambiguities lie behind their terms. Ethologists themselves may not be unduly hindered by these confusions: but their lay readers demonstrably are, particularly when such concepts as 'territory', 'altruism' and 'aggression' are in question.

Preface

What follows is, I hope, an interesting beginning: I have no illusions about its completeness or unanswerability. What any author writes must be interpreted by the reader, and used rather as a stimulus to further thought than a record of unambiguous truth. I hope the enterprise is found enjoyable.

Some of the ideas floated here have also been tried out in papers read in Glasgow, Lampeter, Lancaster and at a UFAW conference at Oxford: I found all comments helpful, especially those of Donald Griffin and Nick Humphrey. I am also grateful to my friends, students and reviewers, particularly to Stephen Bostock, Gillian Clark, William Lyons and Flint Schier.

21 November 1981
University of Glasgow

CONTENTS

Chapter 1

INTRODUCTION

At the close of Chesterton's *The Man who was Thursday* Gabriel Syme, emerging from his vision or adventure, 'could not remember having ever come to at all. He could only remember that gradually and naturally he knew that he was and had been walking along a country lane with an easy and conversational companion.' It is an experience familiar to us all, for we have all (as it were) woken up to find ourselves embroiled in a world where many different creatures compete or work with us, recognize our footsteps and remember pasts that we have forgotten. We live in houses that we did not make, walk roads we did not lay, keep bargains that we never consciously made. Some creatures that we encounter carry faces much like ours, some speak in languages we already know. Others are more mysterious to us, but even these we seem to understand in part.

This is the world in which we live, a world of clouds and trees and people. We do not have to labour to invent for ourselves a concept of such a world, merely on the basis of coloured patches, sounds, smells and pinpricks. The ordinary concept of the world has been built (as it were) behind our backs, over aeons of evolutionary time and in our personal infancies. We do not need to infer the world's existence, nor its most important characteristics, from more basic truths: nothing is borne in on us more forcefully than that there is a world, of greater scope than our experience of it.

Growing conscious of our own existence in the world, we see ourselves confronted by other creatures, and begin to wonder if they are truly what we find ourselves supposing them to be. Do they encounter us as we encounter them? Are their feelings really what we take them to be? The faces that were open to our gaze, expressions of love, anger, fear or doubt, recognized without the aid of reason, come to seem mere masks: the real selves must lie behind those forms, and what could we know of them?

The moment when we come to find the world less obvious than it seemed is the beginning of philosophy. Is there any way in which we can retrieve the unreasoning conviction into which we woke? Once, we had no doubts; now that we can say that John is angry or that Jane is tired, we can also see the possibility that this is false, a merely seeming truth, and how shall we decide?

The beginnings of philosophy, or sometimes of madness: I have tried to explore the connections between these modes of human consciousness elsewhere (18). But also, and in particular, this doubt lies at the beginning of ethology, the study of animal behaviour in its natural setting. Amongst the things we encounter are creatures defined for us as animals (non-human). Even in cities we grow up with them: domestic pets, and birds on the lawn, and (more distantly) the animals we eat, torment, displace. We grow up believing that a dog, for instance, may be angry, hostile or ashamed. We impute to these non-human things all manner of dispositions, feelings, moral qualities that we also assign to men. Sometimes we find ourselves assigning such attributes to whole kinds of animal: sharks are vicious killers, cats cruel, sheep docile. Are we right, in general or in any given case, so to impute such feelings to this class of creature? Or is the case still worse: their masks concealing only nothingness, like suits of armour walking with no occupant?

The inherited conglomerate of belief and fancy has left us this particular problem, for some strands of our tradition make of men something quite other than mere animals. We are things of a different kind, and all our attributions of human thought and feeling to the animals must be intended in some special sense. They do not feel as we feel, think as we think, for we are rational and they are not. It is only a step from this to the conclusion that they do not think or feel at all, are only motions of mere matter, and material for any purpose we may have for them.

The fancy sits uneasily with most of us, for we also feel ourselves to be living creatures much like them. What are animals really like? How far can we trust our own unthinking recognition of their fear, fidelity or cleverness? How far should we accept the impulse to decree a strict division between us and them?

Here then is the issue. How shall we decide? I make no secret that my own vote falls with those who would deny a radical division between 'men' and 'beasts'. I find myself among creatures with many different qualities, 'fellow voyagers in the odyssey of evolution' (59). I trust my ability to grasp the meanings and the moods of creatures with whom I would not interbreed as much, in principle, and no more than I trust my intuitions of my fellow humans' moods: though allowance must be made for the unfamiliar, and for species-specific cues. The moral conclusions that I draw from this I have expounded elsewhere (17), and now mention them only to make clear that I, like any other student of these things, have some convictions that may bias my approach, however detached I strive to be.

That I have my own convictions constitutes one possible source of error. That I must deal with matters beyond my professional competence, another. I am sure that much of ethological research has passed me by; maybe I sometimes repeat long-exploded errors as new-discovered fact. What errors I make should be corrected by those who know better, if they do. But I would ask that my readers with any biological training remember both that what seems error may really be a different interpretation as well-grounded as their own, and that the perils of specialization run both ways. It is unfortunately easy to pick out the biologists in a gathering largely of philosophers: they are the ones who raise sceptical quibbles about any postulate, urge that we never know what anyone else is thinking, that morality is only a matter of inarguable taste, that only what is 'scientifically verifiable' has any meaning. These dogmas, invented by philosophers, have few serious philosophical advocates today, and their constant intrusion into the debate is at least as irritating to philosophers as any error of fact made by philosophers is to practising scientists. The philosopher at a gathering of biologists, by the way, is the one in a state of permanent exasperation that these scientists do not understand their own concepts! We are all inclined to think that we know each other's business better. If this short book does anything to encourage dialogue between our different disciplines it will not have wholly missed its aim.

The province I have chosen to explore is constituted by the impulses and inhibitions, learned and instinctual, that seem to play the part in beasts that morals play in us (whatever that part is) – the morals of Nature, as one might call them. Is this more than a remote and unhelpful analogy? And if it is, what moral can we draw from it? Are there such things as the morals of beasts? Might they be our morals too?

The morals of Nature: not the codes by which Nature itself is guided to produce mammoths and men and thunderstorms. My object here is not so metaphysical. Nature's morals in that sense, if any, are not ours, and what they might be only baffles thought. The morals, or pseudo-morals, or quasi-morals of my enquiry are those, perhaps, acknowledged by individual animals in their lives and works.

It is an ancient puzzle. The almost universal judgement of mankind has been that animals do indeed show love, devotion, righteous anger, shame, that they are governed in part by laws, instinctive and learned. It is natural law that parents care for their children, spare their defeated clan-mates, respect sexual taboos and figures of authority. The claim is not that all sorts of animal do this, nor that all individuals even of a generally 'moral' species do this, but that enough do it, often enough to suggest that their desires are not wholly egotistical. Perhaps the roots of ethical concern were here, and from such natural concern for our defenceless young, or unwillingness to savage our fellows, the moral systems of mankind were raised. This account can be found among the Stoic philosophers of the Hellenistic age, who also declared that men, being rational, were of another sort entirely. Morals began with such animal impulses, but must deny their roots: good men do not let themselves be governed by personal attachment, irrational shames or idiosyncratic loyalties.

The greatest names of our tradition followed this second theme, and thought of *animals* as entirely 'animal'. To be animal, in popular speech inherited from past philosophers, is to be brutal, lustful, violent or (at best) unthinkingly and quite unrealistically affectionate. But the first theme, that the roots of our own morality lay in certain fundamental responses of affection, propriety, loyalty, mercy and self-sacrifice, has had supporters.

In our day, and especially since the theory of evolutionary transformism has become the ruling myth - I do not say the false myth - of educated men, we have come to look again at these our fellows. If we are related, we must surely expect to see analogies or homologies of behaviour (functional or struc-tural resemblances), as well as of anatomy. Some patterns of behaviour not only fill identical roles within the creatures' lives, but are (we must suspect) inherited from some common ancestor. Those who doubt that behaviour is heritable may like to consider love-birds: peach-faced love-birds carry nest ma-terial in their feathers, Fischer's love-birds in their bills. They do not need to learn by imitation. Hybrids, poor unfortunates, get muddled till they find some workable compromise (26). Some behaviour, obviously, is learned, though even in such cases it is likely that there is some inherited propensity which makes some kinds of learning easier than others. Could morals be a different case, sent down from heaven unexpectedly to fill the part vacated by 'animal instinct'? Animals, it has been said, are ruled by instinct or by Nature: men have minds, and must do themselves what Nature itself does for other species. On such a view, there may be rough analogies between animals' behaviour-patterns and human morals, but the mecha-nisms are entirely different.

Such radical breaks are possible, although the scientific

consensus is probably against them. But even if it were not we should not be too eager to postulate such a division here: the hypothesis appeals too readily to human pride, to a strange willingness to think ourselves quite other than the beasts. Those who deny the gap are often thought, even by themselves, to be administering a blow to our pretensions: maternal love is only what birds feel; sexual delight only that figment which drives dinosaurs to mate. As 'animals' have sometimes been defined as 'merely physical', this reduction ends in claiming that some noble emotion is 'only glandular'. Those who would assert the serious value of the emotion so described then feel obliged to claim that this is more than physical, hence more than 'animal', and animals but matter after all.

Myself, I see no reason to be ashamed that I and 'animals' may share the enchantments shed by sexuality, may feel a like protectiveness for small, defenceless things. Equally, I doubt whether all sexual acts, for instance, can really be equated with each other, even in a single species: the bond of greylag geese is the so-called triumph rite, not sex as such (64), and the gander who mates outside his triumph bond is not doing just the same thing as when he mates within it. An adequate description of an act must involve more than a bare account of the events contained within a given period. It must include some account of motivation, function and connection with other acts. In accepting that men and beasts are creatures, very broadly, of the same kind, I do not need to insist that they do all and only the same things.

The matter is complicated by political bias. For some reason those writers who have made most play with the apparent analogies between human and non-human behaviour and motivation have been recognizably right-wing. Animals have been invoked to prove the propriety, or at least the ineluctability, of aggression, hierarchical order, sexual dominance. Commentators move with faintly risible effect from sexual 'division of labour' among the social insects, to role-distinctions amongst hunter-gatherers, to the social arrangements of middle-class America (104). Those of a different persuasion have suspected all such efforts to make contemporary society seem ideal or irreformable. Even to speak of 'human nature' seems to be to earn the name of 'right-wing reactionary' (13).

Some of these criticisms have been off the point. Ethologists, as I shall be showing later, have had a tendency to appropriate words to their own use. The view that there is an innate aggressive drive suggests to some that Lorenz, for example, believes men to be ineradicably murderous, carni-

vorous, prone to war. In fact when Lorenz speaks of aggression
(64) and Fromm of human destructiveness (40) they are speaking of quite different things. On the other hand, ethologists
who have approached the human animal do display, on occasion, a bizarre regression to the worst features of scissors-
and-paste anthropology:

A particular form of greeting bow is practised by Fulah
women. They turn their backsides towards the person
greeted and bow deeply. This behaviour pattern is uncom-
monly reminiscent of the appeasement 'presentation' of
various apes and monkeys. Perhaps this represents the
persistence of a behavioural root. It is certainly noticeable that in Europe on the outside of old porticoes and
city gateways bared buttocks are shown. From Japan I
know protective amulets that show the same thing . . . In
this connection Wickler mentions that in ancient Germa-
nia both men and women stuck their bared bottoms out of
their front doors to propitiate Wotan. In Japan men and
women had to ward off spirits by lining up and parting
their kimonos to show their sexual organs. In this case
there was both appeasement by means of female mating
invitation and a phallic threat to the evil spirits . . . The
principle of linking a phallic threat with female presentation is also seen in the common marmoset of South
America. (31)

Anthropologists trained to see that human culture deploys the
basic stock of gesture, posture, sound in ways not fixed by
heredity are likely to find this about as interesting as the
remark that a given vocable is used in lots of places, and
sometimes means quite different things. But we should not let
exasperation prevent our agreeing that human beings do indeed
share much of their behavioural repertoire, with each other
and with our non-human kin. If ideologues have used ethology
for suspect ends, if sound ethologists have yet made silly
claims, it does not follow that we should abandon all attempt
to see what our non-human kindred do, or what our human
nature may involve. 'Natural moralities', those we share with
other mammals and those peculiar (if such there be) to
creatures of our species, need not be right-wing in effect.
There may be reasons to deny the analogies, but political
idealism need not be one of them.

So much for my preamble. In sorting through the tangled
strands of our inherited conglomerate to find if we can see
what animals are really like, we may expect some help from
professional students of animal behaviour. Some of these

results may serve us well in organizing our own lives, though it would be very rash (for many reasons) to argue from chimpanzee promiscuity, for example, to any moral suitable for human sexuality, or from the territorial behaviour of butterflies to a defence of market capitalism.

Such transitions have not been invented by right-wing biologists, nor by their critics. It has been a tradition with us to use animals as good examples, or as bad. If chimpanzees mate promiscuously, the conclusion has been, variously, that so should we, or else that we must take care lest we be betrayed by our 'animal selves' to conduct unworthy of a gentleman. Where such opposing morals may be drawn, more matters to us than mere information about anthropoids.

More matters than this, but this at least may be of value. If we are to understand the animals with whom we share the world, we need to watch them, interact with them, without too much prejudice. Understanding them, we may also understand ourselves a little more. By seeing what constrains and motivates our kindred we may, perhaps, discover what the morals and manners of the human beasts might be.

Chapter 2

OPPOSITION TO ANIMISM

Animal behaviour is currently studied in many different ways, by those with an immediate practical interest in the creatures as well as by those with more theoretical aims. A great deal of research is conducted in laboratories to see how well the creatures can cope with situations carefully contrived to eliminate as many unwanted variables as may be. Animals are regularly doped, maimed, hampered, frustrated, pained, to see which way, how often, they will jump. Similar experiments, though none so brutal, are tried on human subjects, sometimes with their consent. Some results of this research are relevant to my concerns: in employing them I do not endorse the ethics of employing creatures in such ways. Very little information, if any, is, in my view, of such weight as to excuse such assaults.

But animals are also studied 'in the wild': all students, of course, affect their subject populations in some degree, if only by providing another object in the animals' landscape. Other students may provide food, or even medical attention, or pose puzzles for the animals' solution. Some ethologists and some laboratory scientists are probably disturbing the creatures they study to a very similar extent. But there may still be a real difference of methodological theory. Ethologists aim to see and understand the normal behaviour of their subjects; they aim to fit their observations into a theory of the life-style of the animal, within the setting of neo-Darwinian evolutionary theory, without recourse (or at least without constant recourse) to the creation of artificially varied situations. In this ethologists and social anthropologists share an ideal of careful observation that can be supported in a framework of Aristotelian science.

That is, for some, the trouble. Aristotelian science is popularly equated with the notorious 'Dark Ages', themselves extended to cover the whole of medieval culture. Does not modern science rest on a strict denial of Aristotelian methodology? In place of an appeal to occult entities, to 'natural forces', to customary and intuitive descriptions of phenomena, the founders of modern science insisted on exact description of the results of controlled experiments. Only by changing one thing at a time and noting the changed results can the contribution of individual causes be calculated. Francis Bacon spoke, deliberately, of 'putting Nature to the question' -putting artificial constraints on what may happen. The Baconian scientist hopes to learn precisely from what is unnatural, contrived: the Aristotelian to see what happens 'by nature', where no extraneous constraints pervert the result. Another strand in the tradition is this: since Galileo, scientists have employed ideal models (what, for example, would happen to an unimpeded moving object of a kind we never in fact meet) and seen the actual happenings as modifications of this ideal event. Aristotelians abjured such figments, preferring the observed behaviour of real things to ideal models never fully matched in our world. Again: the modern scientist professes to detest all teleology, all mention of ends, equating it with animism or the will of God. All events are to be described 'objectively', as the motions of pure objects, never as the acts of subjects. Aristotelians, notoriously, think final causes (as health is of medicine, or the adult form of an embryo) are required to understand not only all biology but physics too, and include subjects in their scope.

On these three counts, the self-image of the modern scientist seems to require a firm stand against a backward slide to medieval ways. Has not science, as now understood, proved its worth? All theories that rest on uncontrolled observation (anecdote), that fail to employ ideal models, that use occult entities and final causes, must be anathema. It is noticeable also that such modern science is atomistic, requiring us to think that it is always possible, in principle, to change 'just one thing at a time' and so distinguish individual causes. Students of animal behaviour who are affected by this cultural set must hope always to draw their science a little closer to the ideal of mechanics, and greatly fear to be thought 'animists'. Thus D. O. Hebb, after describing a severely disturbed chimpanzee whom he plausibly analyses as suffering from a repressed sexual attachment to Hebb himself, hurriedly adds that this diagnosis implies nothing about conscious states (47, pp. 245ff.). Tinbergen aims, not wholly consistently, for a similarly aseptic vocabulary (95). Only observable facts of an indefinitely repeatable sort can be admitted. If we use ordinary language at all, it must be with the constant proviso that terms like altruism, aggression, love have very special senses.

The actual merits of this philosophy of science are not, in general, my concern. Nor do I wish to argue whether or not such science has 'proved its worth'. Both points are more debatable, and more obscure, than propagandists usually admit. What does concern me here is whether we must always prefer such forms of science and theory in matters ethological. Students of animal behaviour may feel that I am labouring fairly obvious points, or else attacking straw men. In their commendable attention to details, scientists are not always alive to the general principles involved. What follows is discussion, not attack.

To begin with the end: final causes need not be equated with occult entities, backward causation, or the divine will. To speak of function is not to imagine (save only, sometimes, as an aid to thought) an actual designer of the World Machine. The function of an organ or a behaviour pattern is that consequence without whose general occurrence the organ or behaviour would not have been selected. Such functions are not the same as causes, in our modern sense, nor are they necessarily the goals of individuals.

The confusion of function and goal is one of the most pervasive errors in learned and in popular ethology (75). Richard Dawkins, for example, in what is in any case a fairly unconvincing account of the function of a baby's crying (that predators are thereby attracted who may possibly eat up the baby's siblings), apparently imagines, momentarily, that he is imputing fratricidal motives to the neonate (24): why else does he consider such a suggestion ghoulish? As a guess at the baby's goal it is; as a guess at the evolutionary function of colic (that colicky babies survive better than their siblings, either by getting attention from terrified parents or by achieving the death of their siblings) it is merely ridiculous. It is also, incidentally, an example of the neo-Darwinian's habit of seeing function everywhere. Dawkins is usually fairly careful.

Functions and goals are both important elements of explanation: or at least we need stronger arguments than those of Baconian religion to prove otherwise. Maybe Aristotelians were wrong to speak of ends as explanatory in the context of things' falling or rising; maybe they were mistaken to attribute purposes (conscious attention to such ends) to the celestial spheres or their intelligences (the postulated entities who explain the observed motions of the stars and planets). It does not immediately follow that we are wrong to attribute purposes to people, chimpanzees or bees, nor that we are wrong to identify the evolutionary functions of eyes, the appendix and parental care. Ethologists need not so desperately attempt to give old words new meanings, thus confusing both themselves and others. An Aristotelian teleology provides both for functional analysis and for the admission of conscious goals.

On the other hand, there is also some danger that in

pursuing our efforts to fit animal behaviour into the evolutionary story we shall neglect the influence of mere chance. It is
of course legitimate to try to find evolutionary functions for
any general feature of a kind, but there must be some point
after which it is no longer reasonable to expect success. What
is the evolutionary function of our susceptibility to the common cold? Must every inherited feature have won out against
its rivals in fair contest (not necessarily a bloody contest), or
may some of them be ours simply because some natural
catastrophe happened to leave only a few survivors? If there
were only two or three human beings to survive Ragnarok, and
they happened to have red hair (but did not survive because
they had red hair), should their descendants debate about the
evolutionary function of hair colour? It may be that the very
proper urge to make sense of living creatures in neo-Darwinian
terms has caused some neglect of mere catastrophe and
genetic drift as factors in evolutionary history. This in turn
may explain why some ethologists and sociologists have been
right-wing: they have tended to assume that every feature of
social behaviour has had evolutionary significance, has won
against its rivals. Even if they then remind themselves (and us)
that times and circumstances may have changed, that what
was adaptive may no longer be, there is clearly a strong bias
towards conservatism. If much of our social behaviour is the
product of chance it may more readily be changed.

The use of ideal models, whatever its merits in the
physical sciences, is also of no obvious or universal value in
the biological. Biological organisms are so complex that ideals
can tell us very little of the real creatures. An 'animal
preparation' - that is, a creature restricted, denatured and
sometimes maimed - may sometimes act in ways predictable
by some such simple mechanism. A real creature, even a
laboratory-bred creature in a precisely controlled environment
and receiving a carefully calculated stimulus, will (as the
saying goes) do precisely what it likes. Of course, we can make
guesses about what the animal will do, what it will like, but it
is far from clear that we do so by calculating what an ideal
animal-model would do. Those who actually deal with animals
(zoo-keepers or farmers or laboratory technicians) rely in
practice on our common resources of empathy and understanding (46, 70). It is simply more helpful to be told that a given
creature is sulky or irritable or playful than to be offered a
computer print-out of the behaviour patterns of the Ideal
Whatever (however interesting that may sometimes be).
Sometimes it is useful to see a piece of behaviour as the
product of two or more opposing impulses (courting behaviour

11

as a product of lust and fury, maybe), but an individual's
conduct is never wholly what would thus be expected. Ethologists (and all of us) talk far too much about what 'the wolf'
does, or 'the chimpanzee', thus hiding from ourselves the
actual diversity and unrepeatability of living forms.

I should emphasize that I do not mean to imply that living
creatures are unique in this. It is easy to imagine that non-
living systems are easily replicable, readily predictable, but in
fact it is quite difficult to get experiments to work, even
under laboratory conditions. Things don't work as they should,
sometimes because of factors that cannot be easily identified
or isolated. We expect machines to work with 'machine-like
precision', but know very well that they regularly go wrong. It
would be odd if living creatures did not behave in a similar
way, though they do usually embody the sort of controls that
more sophisticated machines do: when they begin to drift away
from the proper course, they are brought back on target -
though these circuits can go wrong as well.

In short, the machine-model for living systems should not
cause us to expect very much exact predictability. But the
model can of course be useful, at least to our imaginations. If
we conceive the behaviour of an animal as if it were controlled by a hydraulic system (each successive container begins
to fill only when the preceding one is full), we can make the
creature's behaviour vivid to ourselves, and begin to see how
the model would have to be altered to deliver what we observe
of a given creature. Perhaps, as it were, pressure can build up
to activate the next stage even if it is (rationally) quite
inappropriate. These models, if understood merely as models,
can certainly be useful, but we should not imagine that a
creature really is operated by a hydraulic system! What moves
an individual animal may be formally similar, in the broadest
outline, to the model, but in cases where we are naturally
equipped to empathize with the animal we should often do
better to trust our feelings.

If we cannot expect, or dare not decree, that idealizing
methods will in practice be most successful (though they will
often be helpful if we use them carefully) in our dealings with
the biological, what have we to rely on? The question poses
itself also in considering the dogmas of atomism. Can we ever
'change one thing at a time'? What, in these contexts, is one
thing? The least change possible, perhaps. Can we claim that
causation is summative? If A causes B, and C causes D, will A
and C together cause B and D? We have no right to say so. The
adjustment that a system makes to the excision of one part
need not reflect the contribution made by that part when it

was in place. Three-legged dogs can walk. Confronted by such problems in our everyday affairs, we rely, sometimes and undogmatically, upon a grasp of how the system works that need not be (it may be) analysed in summative terms. How else should we have lived so long in this world?

It is really very strange that so much is made of the proven worth of modern science, a methodology (it is supposed) of not much more than three centuries' age. As humans and pre-humans (or so we're told) we have relied on 'intuitive', 'holistic', even 'animistic' methods of comprehending other creatures for several million years. Such few advantages, of practice and of understanding, as some few of us have lately gained from 'the scientific method' would be impossible without that massive and continuing debt to ordinary judgement (71). The claim that it is obsolete is, at least, unnecessarily dismissive.

Our common understanding, finally, need not rely upon creating artificial states, nor torture Nature to reveal the Truth. The idea that a creature's nature is revealed most usefully in extreme, unusual, contrived conditions is surely odd. I may not know just what my friends, or I myself, would do if starved or beaten, blinded or made sick. It does not follow that I do not know them well, still less that their eventual (it may be) betrayal of a noble cause reveals them as unfaithful from the start. Extremities may try the soul, but they may also break it. To break a thing to find out what it is, is far too paradoxical a method to be adopted wholesale. The Ik (a tribe of Ugandan hunters driven from their former range who behave with extraordinary callousness to their own kind) do not show us 'human nature stripped of its veneer of civility', the real basis on which we must raise up our laws. The Ik are broken men (99). Our common understanding, patently, has perils. Often enough we find that what we had attributed to a friend was only our projected consciousness, not the friend's at all. If this occurs even between friends, of a common species and culture, how much more easily between different kinds of cultures? *Pace* David Hume, a peacock's gait does not prove him proud (though he may be) (49), and beasts may often have quite different goals from us. But it is an overreaction to insist that all description be as purely 'behavioural' as possible, that terms imputing humanly recognizable emotion (such as 'anger' or 'threat') are to be purified and defined solely in terms of what subsequent movements occur in the subject animals. It is of course very difficult to maintain such an antiseptic attitude, especially when the terms used have colloquial meanings. But the attempt is made, perhaps under the impression that an 'objective' description (that is, one free of our projections) must be also an 'objective' one (that is, one that treats the creatures studied purely as objects). 'Communication', for animal scientists, tends (reasonably enough, once consciousness is left out of consideration) to cover everything from the dissemination of hormones by social amoebas to the signalling systems of the higher primates (sometimes including humans) (29). Such 'communication' is to be understood purely as a causal process, linking emitter and receiver in such a way that subsequent motions are statistically predictable.

This approach is sometimes made even to human behaviour, including verbal communication. No reference need ever be made to any inner consciousness, or conscious purposes. All that matters is what is perceptible, and all that is perceptible are the outward motions of our bodily frames. To infer the existence of an inner (i.e. subjective) life would, at best, be unscientific, and at worst meaningless.

If this is so, our whole moral vocabulary needs to be purified, or purged. For common language clearly relies on the assumption of 'inner life' and 'conscious purpose'. It is difficult for me to take this theme seriously. Those who claim not to be conscious, or to be conscious only in the purified sense that they can be relied upon to react in certain ways to stimuli, cannot be telling the truth. What is said may be true (it would be if a tape-recorder said it), but it cannot be told as the truth, since only conscious creatures can tell, claim, purpose anything.

Pure behaviourism, whether it allows a grotesque anomaly in the case of the self (so that I am conscious and no one else is) or insists that nothing, not even the speaker, is conscious, is not seriously defended by anyone (though there are those who deny that there is any such substantial thing as consciousness). It is a necessary assumption of scientific or any other enquiry that we can collaborate with our fellows, that they are conscious and purposive beings much like ourselves, who can recognize obligations of accuracy and rational enquiry. Science is an activity of conscious beings, and if there are no such creatures, science (as commonly understood) is an impossibility. Efforts to build up a genuinely non-personal science are unlikely to be successful.

Cartesian behaviourism (named after its most famous, though hesitating advocate René Descartes), which allows that human adults at any rate are conscious, inner-directed entities, is in practice a more popular option. Animals are to be described behaviouristically, not only as a methodological device to delay too ready an assumption of intuitive insight,

14

but as an ontological dogma. It is important that we should distinguish the weaker from the stronger thesis. Ethologists may employ the weaker as a matter of professional discipline: that animals should be described without too much of empathy, solely in terms of what they 'do'. They do not need to adopt the stronger claim, that animals have no 'inner life', no purposes of a human kind. Once again, there may be arguments to convince us of this, but official ethological practice is not one of them.

But what can be said even for the practice? Does it not rest on a very strange equation of 'what is perceptible' with the merely 'physical' (where this is understood very roughly as what has weight and spatial dimensions)? Surely we can perceive a creature's anger or fright or purpose? To insist that all we ever really perceive is a creature's bristling, cowering, crouching or the rest seems absurd. Why should we accept this claim?

Are we bound to? If I can make mistakes (as I can) about what a creature is feeling, I cannot have directly seen the feeling: the feeling that I claimed to see cannot be what I saw - for it does not, as such, exist. What I saw was a set of motions, and thence I mistakenly inferred a real feeling.

But this is a familiar, and naive, version of the so-called 'argument from illusion', the supposed proof that we can never rely on our senses because they can be tricked (which has had a very bad press amongst philosophers in recent years). I can be mistaken also about what a thing is: I can mistake a coiled rope for a serpent. Does it follow that all I 'really' saw was a set of coloured patches from which I mistakenly inferred the presence of a real thing? And should I conclude that in future I will never speak of serpents, ropes, trees, people or plaster dummies (except as shorthand expressions for an indefinitely large list of sensory experiences)?

There have been thinkers who drew, in theory, this conclusion, and so vanished from the ordinary sphere of discourse. The obvious retorts are that my evidence that I am sometimes mistaken is precisely that I am not always mistaken, that the whole notion of seeing is drawn from the public realm in which we *see* stones and trees and people, that indeed all our vocabulary (including terms used by solipsists to describe their private sensa) is drawn from the public realm. We perceive creatures in the world; we perceive them as, precisely, doing things, and our perceptions cannot be isolated from our awareness (sometimes but not always erroneous) of their purposes. Of course we sometimes make mistakes; of course we can be tricked; of course we should be careful when we have good reason to think that some disturbing factor is present (a deep-seated prejudice or an experimental psychologist). It does not follow that we can never with perfect accuracy and justice say that we can see that someone is angry.

The whole notion of an inner and radically imperceptible life, disjoined from the outer and publicly perceived 'physical' life, is in large part a device of philosophy. It has its uses. But when animal scientists are so far indoctrinated as to believe that anyone who speaks of an animal's purposes or inner life is an unscientific mystic (104) it is time to call a halt. 'Minds' are not, for most philosophers, imperceptible entities weirdly connected with perceptible bodies. We have as much right to claim knowledge of people's minds as of their bodies. Both can be placed on the far side of an epistemological divide, but both are, in principle, open to public view. Both are describable in colloquial language which, having been developing for several millennia to serve very subtle ends, is enormously more versatile a tool than the constructions of scientists or philosophers. Ethologists are making use of this tool, however ineptly, when they conclude that an apparently purposive piece of behaviour is not really so. Thus Lorenz, observing a young starling going through a whole fly-catching and consuming routine in the absence of any fly, concludes that the behaviour, which would have seemed so purposive if there had been a fly to be caught and eaten, was actually automatic (86).

This inference is, as it stands, invalid (for there is no obvious reason why we should not think that the bird is playing or pretending), but the general point is a fair one: if someone does just the same things when there is obviously no external goal to be gained by doing so, then it is likely that the behaviour is not adopted as a means to that (impracticable) goal. The more casual and unmotivated the act, the less we see it as a purposive one (though this does not preclude its having a purpose the agent has forgotten). Again, whereas some people marry in order to set up house in order to have children in order to have someone to care for them in their old age (and the list of further goals could be extended), others merely marry, and then want to set up house, and then want children, and so on. The extent to which we plan for our futures, do one thing (or do without one thing) in order to obtain some further goal, is very variable. It is likely enough that even those non-human animals most akin to us do not look far ahead: the coherence and efficiency of their life patterns rests rather on the successive emergence of local and immediate goals. A hunting wasp will not want to seal the nest until she has deposited a caterpillar in it, but these acts are not directed as means to the end that her offspring be well-fed and housed (for she seals the nest even if the caterpillar and her egg have been removed, and she is in a position to be aware of this).

These discriminations lie within our ordinary sphere of discourse. And it is this which is perhaps our age's greatest contribution to philosophical enquiry, that the enquiring mind is not at a distance from the public world. Descartes believed that the proper route to knowledge was to cut himself off from all ordinary belief and natural engagement in the world. By asking what he could logically doubt he hoped to find some certainty on which to build. Perhaps he successfully established his own existence, but if he did, he did not establish any indubitable route from his certainty that he existed to any justified belief that he existed as a bodily organism in the ordinary world. Such radical scepticism leaves one marooned in total solipsism – or not even there, for the whole notion of a person's existing through time as the owner of thoughts and feelings begins to lose its content. If I cannot identify other people, what can I identify myself as? More recent philosophy has concluded both that we should not seek logical indubitability as the sole ground for justifying our beliefs, and also that I am essentially a participant in a community. I am not certain (still less 'logically certain') of my own being and then by difficult degrees convinced of the world's existence, and my friends'. I learn to use personal and egoistic language by communicating with others. The foundation of our scientific enterprise is the community of mindful organisms, creatures that are responsive, enquiring, calculating. We begin, in fact, as social mammals, not as disembodied intelligences.

It is of course possible to entertain very general doubts about the veracity of our experience. Within our universe of discourse there are physical things existing independently of our experience: we do not suppose that material objects exist discontinuously, and only when perceived. But all our observations are compatible with just this view, that the existence of material things lies in their being perceived, that the truth of an assertion amounts to the fact that we would seriously and finally perceive and say it is *true*. The question whether material things or minds *really* exist is a metaphysical problem, not a scientific one. Whether and how we can gain a rational assurance that our universe is not wholly out of touch with what is real is a problem for another day (18). As Aristotle declared, it is not the business of the natural scientist to defend the fundamental axioms of his craft: that

17

there is a universe to be investigated, and that our perceptions of it are not wholly false (1).

One last attempt to down the 'animists' (so called): do they not multiply entities beyond necessity? That there are indeed material things of such and such a kind does provide an explanation, limited but useful, of the phenomena. If we can do the job of predicting what will happen next without recourse to any additional things such as purposes, intentions, desires or inner images, is it not otiose to drag in mental entities or events? It may seem that both materialism and a full-scale spiritualism (which denies material and affirms mental entities and causes) have the edge over 'animism'. We should only mention minds when the purely material account is quite unworkable. But once again, the animist need not suppose that 'minds' are an addition to the world of material things: mindful entities are just those creatures who consciously respond, communicate and purpose in characteristic ways. We should not postulate unobserved entities without good reason (who does?); equally we should not eliminate standing features of our universe without good reason. A spurious simplicity of description which is often of less predictive power than standard character-sketches does not constitute a good enough reason. The question between the 'animist' and the 'objectivist' (so called) is not how many entities there are, but what sort. The onus must be on the 'objectivists' (a tendentious title) to prove their case. That a thunderstorm is, after all, no conscious entity is plausible enough, for it makes no response to our overtures: that people, or chimpanzees, or cats are not truly conscious is a claim too grand for scientists to make.

18

Chapter 3

INTELLIGENCE AND LANGUAGE

Instinct and intelligence

The claim of Stoic philosophy was that animals might behave *as if* they had reason, but were really moved only by Nature. Thomists have similarly insisted that an animal 'non agit, sed agitur': does not act, but is acted on. This notion has descended to our own day as the dogma that any sign of 'intelligent' behaviour on the part of the non-human is purely instinctual: no proof of individual cleverness or conscious purpose. To some this has seemed a renewed appeal to unobservable causes, and a pseudo-explanation. To say that pigeons find their way home 'by instinct' is to say nothing intelligible about how they find their way home.

But the concept has more depth to it than this. Instinctual modes of behaviour are such behavioural patterns as the individual creature needs neither to learn nor to invent. Spiders do not try out web-making as one strategy among many freely imagined possibilities, nor need they copy an older spider's expertise. Of some birds (not all) it is true that they do not need to copy older birds to reproduce a species-specific call. Nor can we suppose that they coincidentally settle upon a freely imagined sequence of notes from a theoretical infinity of such calls. Spiders and birds and other creatures have certain behavioural patterns which are as much a part of their inheritance as their growing of eyes or feathers. It does not follow that individuals do not improve their own performance, nor that there are no communal, culturally transmitted elements of their eventual behaviour. A chaffinch reared in isolation will produce a highly restricted, schematized version of the performance of his wild cousins. Other distinctions must be noted: is a particular behavioural development, normally occurring at a particular age, determined solely by internal causes, or is it cued by an external event, or copied from a companion? Among the more social animals all three factors are doubtless important, and not readily distinguished. Is a young mother cat reproducing the mothering techniques she experienced as a kitten, or was it merely necessary that she be mothered for the appropriate internal mechanism to be started, or would she mother her kittens anyway?

'Instinctual' patterns need not be unintelligent. The opposition between instinct and intelligence is misplaced: intelligence is shown in a grasp of the features of a situation relevant to the animal's purposes, an ability to find satisfactory solutions to perceived problems, or to recognize a suggested solution as a good one. These abilities could not exist without a sturdy foundation of instinctual perceptions and techniques. We are very fortunate that we do not have to invent the notion of a language for ourselves, and could not possibly acquire the ability to speak a particular mothertongue without an innate ability to pick out certain sorts of patterns from the sounds that surround us. None the less, different human individuals may show more or less ability in this matter (and be rated correspondingly higher or lower on verbal intelligence tests).

'Intelligence' is indeed a highly suspect notion when supposed to be a single variable testable in relatively simple ways. Before applying one and the same test (e.g. the successful running of a maze) to creatures of different kinds and backgrounds we should be careful whether we know what those kinds are. Rats do not need to be enticed to learn the turnings of a maze: they readily, and for obvious evolutionary reasons, internalize quite complex mazes. They do not, on the other hand, appear to recognize each other as individuals. Squirrels are likely to do better than dogs at a test requiring them to 'go the wrong way' before they can reach a desired object well in their line of sight. It does not follow that squirrels are in general more 'intelligent' than dogs: rather, different species find different problems easy; solutions will occur to them more readily, sometimes without even any full awareness of the problem.

Is this the point? Practical intelligence is perhaps largely instinctual: animals are equipped (from birth, from some age, from the experience of a cue-event) to solve their problems in one or a few ways. If these solutions do not work they will begin to try them again, or act in a confused and random fashion. In extreme cases, where enterprising psychologists have forestalled all imaginable solutions, they will perhaps retreat into something like a catatonic trance. Real intelligence is shown in an ability to transcend all past solutions, to invent a new technique entirely *de novo*. Such intelligence, it is said, is shown by men, but not by animals.

The case is not so clear. How does 'confused' behaviour differ from a desperate search for new solutions? If it is really confused, resting (as it seems) on no theoretical model of the situation, is that not a merit when the animal lacks any knowledge of the true situation and is trying to find out? When our ordinary solutions do not work, our ordinary understanding

Intelligence and language

has been challenged and we must perforce relapse upon some other technique. Trial and error is not unknown. Baconian scientists should not find the confused behaviour of their animal subjects all that unfamiliar. Animals, unfortunately, cannot win. If they maintain some hypothesis despite initial failure, they are stupid; if they strike out at random in hopes of doing something right, they are still stupid.

Sometimes we blame them for their ignorance. If we incline to call rats intelligent when they decline to accept a speciously attractive bait, the label is hurriedly withdrawn when it is found that they will also avoid genuinely nutritious substances that have arrived too suddenly. This is not intelligent discrimination, but mere (programmed) fear of novelty: we would choose differently.

But why is such a fear of novelty a proof of unintelligence? When it is displayed by young human children it may exasperate their well-intentioned elders, but rats have no reason to think us humans well intentioned. They live in a world where everything is dangerous until proved otherwise, where the causes of events are irremediably occult. It is a sensible and discriminating caution to wait and see. When faced by Warfarin, which kills quite slowly, rats who would try anything once to see what it was like would soon be dead. If rats were as intelligent as we are, we would have killed them all off long ago (30)!

But perhaps our intelligence does not rest entirely on the accumulated results of our trials and errors. When we humans find our ordinary techniques failing us, we relapse upon more subtle models. If the lights fail, we check the bulbs, the switches, the electricity board's programme of economies. Only when these superficial checks fail to render the thing intelligible do we resort to higher-order speculation: are the demons angry with us, have the 'laws of nature' flipped? In seeking new, creative explanations when old customs fail it sometimes seems that truly creative scientists or scholars somehow get 'behind the scenes'. We do not always operate by trial and error but by an intuitive grasp of what things must be like which seems to go beyond anything we could ordinarily have learnt. Of course, some sort of evolutionary account of this ability can be given; we are descended from a host of creatures who, by and large, guessed right. Our guesses enshrine the trials and errors of our ancestors. It is difficult not to wonder whether these abilities do not themselves transcend anything that could be needed to improve the survival chances of our progeny. Practical intelligence will usually be advantageous, but why should a capacity to calculate atomic diameters, compose fugues or devise philosophical riddles be required? It seems likely that the chief skills bred in us, apart from practical intelligence of a kind indistinguishable from the problem-coping capacities of other kinds, are ways with words. Modern cosmology, including evolutionary theory and ethology itself, is a by-product of our story-telling and our rhetoric, our capacity to imagine things we do not immediately experience (18).

But that is by the way. The relevant suggestion here is that the intelligence we have and animals do not is the capacity to tell another story than the one immediately forced on us, to tell a story that is often, strangely, true - or at any rate a helpful fiction. This suggestion requires a further study of the ways of language, but it is at least worth noting that (some) animals do show some capacity to work in relatively novel ways. The chimpanzees who fit two sticks together to reach for a bunch of bananas can be dismissed as working with the ordinary tools of their environment (though students have usually suggested that the apes had a moment of insight). But what of the macaque who found out how to separate wheat from sand by throwing handfuls of the two combined into the sea? This involved an extension of established ways as impressive, in its setting, as most scientific advances.

In sum, it looks as if some animals do dream up new solutions, even if the range from which they choose is determined by the patterns familiar to their kind. Cases adduced to show that no animals are intelligent, never adapt their behaviour to their situation to achieve their goals in ways that show some theory of how the world works, are not wholly convincing. Sometimes we have mistaken, it may be, their goals; sometimes we have neglected some simple point which makes the act they wish to do impossible for them - gibbons who failed to pull their food towards themselves by hauling on strings could not, it turns out, get their hands round the string (53).

Desires and beliefs

Sometimes we have mistaken their goals. This indeed constitutes one of the crucial difficulties in ethology. If a male robin will attack a red feather in preference to a rival robin whose red patch is concealed, does not that show a lack of sense? If a female hunting-wasp will painstakingly seal the nest from which, as she must see, her eggs have been removed, does this not prove stupidity? Must such actions not simply be mechanical responses, and a sign that no intelligence is here at work?

22

The robin's behaviour, of course, has obvious analogies with our own. An avian anthropologist might similarly wonder that we can be moved by schematic representations of, for example, male or female shapes. We do not, save under considerable stress, treat such pictures quite as we would treat a real person in the flesh, but we may well sometimes prefer a picture of appropriate kind to a present person whose character is obscured. We do not need to think ourselves therefore mechanical.

But there is a deeper point. To assume that the robin or the wasp is stupid is to assume that we know what he, what she is trying to do. If the wasp is trying to hatch eggs, her technique is poor: but is she? Or does she just enjoy sealing nests (at this moment of her career)? Is the robin seeking to drive off an intruder? If so, his discrimination is ineffective: but perhaps he dislikes red. Evolutionary function and individual goal are not the same. Should we find that surprising? Moralists have sometimes objected to the use of contraceptives, but no one lists such use as proof that humans are unintelligent.

We cannot discover a creature's desires and belief simultaneously. I must postulate the one in order to identify the other. A desire for a drink implies a belief that the cup being reached for holds something worth the drinking; a belief that it holds poison implies a desire to die. In order to understand an alien (human) tongue we need to assume that its speakers have desires and attitudes much like ours. Where we have reason to believe that they do not, our understanding of what they say is limited. The problem is not that such terms as 'desire' and 'drive' or 'belief' and 'intelligence' are vague and ill-defined (3): it is that they function as the two dimensions of an area - if we know the one, we can calculate the other. Squids, if their vertical lobe is destroyed, will no longer follow a fish around a corner: has their desire or their wit been weakened?

If desires cannot be identified independently of beliefs, we have at last an argument for doubting that animals have (identifiable) desires. Do they, what do they, *believe*? In ordinary life we do not doubt that dogs believe that their master's at the door, that there's a cat outside, that they've done something wrong (?) (8). These are certainly the beliefs that they must have if their actions are to stem from the desires we usually suppose they have. We may doubt that they could believe that Dante wrote the *Purgatorio*, or even that their master will be back in ten days' time (though the latter is not, it seems to me, impossible). But other beliefs we are sure they have. Are we right? And if we are wrong, can we not suppose that they have desires, or feel emotions either?

Again: some feelings do themselves involve beliefs. Anger, as we understand that term, is more than growing hot and clenching fists and threatening aggressive action. Anger is, in part, a state of believing that one has been wronged. If dogs cannot believe, can they be angry?

And finally, to desire something is to believe that something will satisfy one's need. An unformed restlessness, even if it will achieve quiescence in some outcome of the movements it engenders, is not strictly a desire. Without beliefs, non-human animals have no desires (39). Having no desires, they feel no distress or satisfaction, neither pain nor pleasure. They are, after all, the dummies that Descartes supposed.

This conclusion is counter-intuitive, particularly since it also applies to human infants. These too are not distressed by tumbles, loneliness or wind; they have no beliefs, find nothing distressing, desire no end to their unrest and are not angry with their parents for so failing to attend upon their wishes. To believe all this – except, perhaps, of the extremely young – is quite beyond most of us.

But of course the fact that we cannot, or cannot easily, believe something does not prove it false. If we are to deal with the argument I have outlined we must decide whether it is true that animals have no beliefs, or why it might be true. To claim that they do may seem to some to be a regression to the level of traditional anecdote: dogs who reason that their quarry has not gone *here*, so must have gone *there*, and elephants who delay their careful revenges, and all such (allegedly) fabulous beasts. There is indeed a strand of popular thought which treats all beasts as people in disguise, attributing to them all possible devices of intellect and imagination. In other ages it may be well to insist that their ways are not ours, that they may not (and probably do not) carry out long schemes of revenge or fealty. But is that truly the chief danger now, that we should think them people dressed in feather or fur or scale? Why are we warned so often not to commit the 'Clever Hans' fallacy (87)? Hans was a horse who seemed able to solve simple sums, tapping to the appropriate number with his hoof. Only very careful control experiments revealed that he was only tapping until the humans who were present gave him his cue to stop. To any unbiased witness it must surely seem a much more difficult and complex task to detect the subtle cues the humans unconsciously gave, but the episode has since been a perennial warning not to attribute human intelligence to beasts. Of course we should not: each species has its own intelligence. But if the consequence of denying all thought to beasts is to remove their sentience, and our infants' too, we should consider our reasons for doing so carefully.

Why should beasts not have beliefs? If to believe is simply to behave in such a way as would be silly, granted their immediate goals, were the content of the notional belief not true, then beasts believe. Such belief may be (need not be) unconscious, as is my belief that water is drinkable without undue harm. All sorts of things I obviously do believe even if I never speak them, even if I deny them: I count on their being true, or at least if they are not true my behaviour is ill-advised.

Other beliefs I have in the sense that if I were asked a question that is what I'd say (usually): that is how I believe that Athens is in Greece or that Aristotle is the Master of them that know. Such verbal belief is not open to beasts, with the possible exception of such chimpanzees and gorillas as have learnt a little American Sign Language ('Ameslan') (62). Such verbal belief, like the unconscious belief revealed in what I do, is dispositional. The beliefs that seem more relevant to the argument against desire are occurrences, constituted not by what the believer would do or say, but by what attitude he now takes to the content of the supposed belief. To believe in this sense is to affirm as true. To affirm as true is to reject its opposite as false; to affirm as true is to commit oneself, to bind oneself to accept whatever follows by strict logic from that postulated truth. If I say that all squares are rectangular, but fail to deny that some squares aren't, or else allow myself the liberty of saying that this square is not, then I cannot be said seriously to believe my first remark. Belief, in short, is an attitude of commitment to the contents of beliefs, labelled 'propositions' by philosophers. If this is so then non-human animals can only believe, in this strong sense, if they can have such attitudes to propositions. The difficulties are both that beasts perhaps cannot promise or commit themselves, and also that it seems unclear how they can know which proposition they have an attitude to if they cannot express it in words. If I cannot articulate the cat's being on the mat how can I have any attitude to that?

Such strong belief neither beasts nor infants have, most probably. But is it clear that such is required by the earlier argument against their desires or emotions? After all, Pyrrhonian sceptics, whose judgment about everything is in perpetual suspense, may not *believe* that what they are inclined to feel is true. They make no promises, and play their games. It has even been argued that belief is a sophisticated social custom, which should not be invoked in descriptions of other and more 'primitive' societies (74). Is it obvious that people in general do believe that what they believe is true? Do they, in believing one thing, consciously commit themselves to believing what follows from that thing?

Again: are all beliefs really *de dicto* (about the statement)? Are not some *de re* (about the thing)? A belief *de dicto* would be an attitude towards the proposition that the cat is on the mat. A belief *de re* would be about the cat. In expressing such a belief in verbal form we would be bound to admit that what we believe about the cat is that she's on the mat. But an unexpressed belief about the cat is simply an expectation, when the cat or an image of the cat is in our view, of finding her on the mat. This need not involve any attitude towards a proposition or even a verbal formula, simply a readiness to find the cat there, a having-it-in-mind before we reach the place.

Such a belief as this, *de re* and without committal, seems enough to answer the difficulties raised before. Healthy squids believe the fish is round the corner simply in that they expect to find the fish there, not in that they think that it is true the fish is there, and that those who disagree are wrong. That is how a human infant believes there is a face behind the cloth, and so plays peekaboo.

Language

It is even possible that we should attribute some grasp of logic to non-verbal animals (human and non-human). It is at least difficult to see how a human infant, or Premack's chimpanzee Sarah, could acquire any competence in the use of logical symbols if those symbols did not name distinctions and relationships of which the creature was already aware, which she already employed (56). Of course, once words have entered the picture a far greater range and subtlety is possible. In the field of numbers we can recognize, and some beasts can recognize, patterns up to seven or eight without need for words. It would surely be surprising if at least some animals apart from us did not grasp some relationships of the sort we formalize in mathematics and in syllogistic. How would they survive without? However did our ancestors acquire an alien gift?

It is unnecessary here to take an extreme position. Some commentators have so widened the scope of such terms as 'communication', 'memory' or 'purpose' that even atoms may communicate, remember and intend – thus allowing hard-line materialists to sound exactly like panpsychists. Treating such things as purely physical, causal processes, they leave the way open for such experiments as this: flatworms are trained to swim a maze (itself a questionable claim), then chopped up and fed to other flatworms, who supposedly then learn the maze much faster. As Efron remarks, few computer scientists would plan to programme a new computer by scattering the debris of an older one into the computer's case! Conceptual confusion breeds inept experiment (29). On the other hand commentators are so irritated by neglect of the intentional element in communication (and in consciousness) that they insist that beasts do not in any real sense think, communicate or bear things in mind: they only respond to particular stimuli in particular ways.

But though communication is intentional (that is, one creature intends to bring about a change in another by causing a recognition of that intention), it does not follow that animals don't communicate. Our own infants can convey their meanings well enough, and are enraged at parental incomprehension, well before they have an active grasp of language. Cases are recounted of, say, chimpanzees' communicating with each other to deceive, and so entrap, their prey. Most of such non-verbal communication must be protreptic and not assertoric: concerned with conveying mood or menace or invitation, not with making statements about things in the world. Our own system of communication allows us (even compels us) to talk about enduring objects, and to recognize the same (propositional) content under many forms: if I hit you, then you are hit by me, and someone has hit you, and I've hit somebody, and I've done something to you, and a few hours later you're still the one I hit. It does not appear, so far, that non-human and non-verbal systems can, in general, cope with this complexity of inference. And of course there has been a long tradition of thought which suggests that our habit of objectifying bits and pieces, aspects, of the world, of recognizing one and the same thing under several transformations, of rejecting contradictions, constitutes a partial, and perhaps erroneous, approach to living. Even without this metaphysical hesitation (which I do not wholly endorse) we can remember that much of our communication is still concerned with status (our own, our audience's), mood, encouragement and threat. When we are living most intensely our language is all 'Um' and 'Yum' and 'Ah' (barring only that strange form of life, a scholar's intense thought). We do not cease to be conscious and appetitive beings when we cease to worry about stating facts.

It may be that other animals do have some systems that

allow them to speak of things in the world. Vervets have a system of calls whereby they call attention to specific sorts of predator (88). There is evidence, unsurprisingly, that rhesus monkeys (say) conceive themselves to move within a stable world where objects can be put down and rediscovered where they were before. Rats, as I have mentioned, can so learn a maze that they can find alternative routes to a goal when their first route is blocked. What seems to be lacking in this - though work with wolves may some day prove us wrong (44) - is any common code, whereby one creature's cognitive map can be aligned with another's. One beast can get others to go somewhere, but only by chasing or pushing or enticing or exciting them, not by saying 'There's a red deer by the second oak tree on the left once you're past the rocks.'

The one possible exception that has so far been studied is the 'language' of bees (61). Such social insects have long fascinated men and been regarded as the sharers of that same light that men are heirs to, but being insects they are not the obvious candidates for an intelligence like ours. Insects are quite other things than us, reminders that evolution is not necessarily directed to the production solely of the human mind. In appearance and behaviour insects remind industrial men of machines. We might almost say they think of each other as machines: witness those ants that are transformed into walking larders, or the pupae that are used to sew leaves together to make a nest, or the 'queen' transformed into an egg factory for her sisters' genetic advantage (on which more below). We do not expect such creatures to be much like us; indeed we hope they're not - if the insects were anything like small humans, or small mammals, their lives would be a nightmare. Unsurprisingly, humanistic scholars have chosen to insist that bees cannot possibly communicate, because they cannot possibly intend any effects of their behaviour and do not understand the 'messages' we can read in what they do. But such a dogmatic insistence goes beyond what we are entitled to claim. Even if there were no reason to believe that bees communicate, that would not itself justify a claim that there couldn't be. In the absence of a divine revelation on the subject we would have to admit to ignorance (43).

In fact, there is a fair amount of quite suggestive, though not conclusive evidence. Incoming bees who have located a source of nectar perform a dance upon the face of the honeycomb which subtends the same angle to the vertical as the correct line of flight does to the sun. The value of the source seems to be indicated by the intensity and persistence of the bee's dance, and rival bees can be persuaded. Moreover, bees appear to retain some memory overnight of the source's location, and adjust their early morning dance to the sun's position: that is, they refer to yesterday's nectar. These operations do constitute a strong analogy, at least, with human communication, though over a very limited range of acts and objects. If bees have cognitive maps of their environment, and a code whereby their individual maps are aligned, and treat each other both as possible audience and possible informants, it is difficult to see what else could be needed. Do they tell each other stories of superb flower beds when they rouse a little from their winter doze? Do they form factions? Probably not: bees, perhaps, are a little too well organized. What have they to talk about? We can guess (it is a guess) that they are more content with their life, unadorned, than we with ours. They do not take the sort of sideways look at life that we do, and have not elaborated the worlds upon worlds of art and history and science that allow us a way to rebuild customary life - or so we guess.

Bees, so far, are a special case. Other social insects seem to rely on chemical, presumably unconscious cues to regulate the nest's behaviour. Termites build their houses not co-operatively, and to a common goal, but by the aggregation of local endeavours. At the first stage they deposit clay at random over the area; some piles, growing a little taller, stimulate the termites to add their pellets here; if two piles are sufficiently close together, the builders will eventually curve them to meet in an arch. And so, by successive stages, the house is built. This much does seem to be the kind of thing quite simple automata could do, though we may be missing aspects of the operation, and may (as always) be misled by the specious simplicity of the investigator's description. What actually happens may be more obscure than this idealized account suggests. Still, it looks as if termites give less sign of being communicative beasts than bees.

Those creatures with whom we share a common heritage of amniotic or mammalian life communicate more perspicuously. Like us, they communicate by scowls and contracted pupils, turned heads and growls and hunched shoulders. We can be misled by this, as we can be misled by the conventional signals of another human culture. A notorious case: the bared-teeth chattering of chimpanzees, employed as light relief in tea commercials, is no sign of happy gossiping, but of fright. This is one good reason why ethologists have preferred as non-interpretative a description of the observed behaviour as possible - but this should only be a prelude to offering (as here) a more accurate interpretation. Such signs may often be

ritualized enactments of the acts that they threaten: relatively schematized, and detached from the conclusion of the act.
Animals may communicate their status by 'threatening' or
'cringing', conveying what they might do, if pushed, by half-
doing it. The threat itself may be stylized, almost perfunctory:
a dominant (male) wolf may merely raise his lip, reminding his
subordinate what an impressive display he could mount, how he
would fight, if he so chose. Some ethological accounts, perhaps, are too jargon-ridden here. Leonard Williams, a human
well acquainted with woolly monkeys, justly remarks that
much of what is said about 'appeasement rituals' refers to
nothing but the expression of friendship (102). Raising hats and
shaking hands may be appeasement rituals in historical origin
('See, I've no weapon, and I unshield my head'), but that is not
what they are now. The regular touching, patting, embracing,
grooming of chimpanzees may be a mechanism for defusing
tension, but the ritual is not mechanical.

Not mechanical: but is it purposive? Expressive behaviour,
after all, that conveys knowledge of my state, and may
transform the mood of my audience, is not always intended to
convey that knowledge or effect that transformation. Its
evolutionary function may be to do so, but that may not be my
intention: I may not have any intention in the matter at all, or
may even intend to conceal my state (unsuccessfully). Sometimes my face expresses more than I wish - though it may also
be that I intend rather more to be noticed than I say I do.
Sometimes I wish to conceal my anger; sometimes I wish to be
seen concealing anger; sometimes I wish to convey my anger.
Purely expressive behaviour, without thought of how that
behaviour affects others (if there is such a thing: we seem to
learn even pain-behaviour in social circumstances), is not
strictly communicative, though it may tell its audience a lot.
Can we decide this question in the case of beasts?

One piece of evidence might be the cat that lazily lifts
one lip, closes one eye, but shows no wish to fight (65). But a
more significant phenomenon is that labelled 'meta-communi-
cation'. It is possible for a 'higher animal', at any rate, to sign
that subsequent signs are meant in play, not genuine threats
but games. Or that they're meant for someone in particular, or
meant to be taken seriously, as from a dominant creature to a
subordinate. In signalling about signals the animal seems to
give us reason to believe that those signals are not purely
expressive. Other interpretations are possible, but not compel-
ling. The sign for 'Play' instructs, does not express; the signs
that follow are part of a game with rules. Those rules can be

exploited: a chimpanzee can encourage youngsters to play, and thereby get a chance to steal their food (58).

It may be that it is from this capacity deliberately to take on other roles that our capacity to be aware of multi-valent objects in the world arises. Instead of a world of practical possibilities, where objects exist only as elements of action (food, rival, sex), we are confronted by a world of separate objects that can have many meanings, many uses.

One feature of such communication that is worth mentioning is that it is highly context-dependent. A creature's understanding of what is to be conveyed rests heavily on the concrete realities of the situation. Meaning is not dependent on a single stream of symbols that can be excerpted from their context and understood identically whenever they are used. It is therefore hardly surprising that such chimpanzees as have been taught American Sign Language are confused when the signs are made without the signer's full affective attention: smell, posture, situation are at odds with the gestures. Human children would be similarly distressed if they were told things in quite inappropriate tones of voice. So, indeed, are we all. Signs take their meaning from their context: 'presentation' may be an invitation to mate, or a gesture of respect toward a dominant. Even if there is a primary medium of communication (as sounds, or gestures), it is assisted by other features of the signer, and of the situation in which the communication is taking place.

To this extent it is fair to say that even the most expert of non-human language users, Ameslan apes, seem to lack an understanding of signs in the abstract. But it is far from clear that any such understanding is possible even for us. A sentence shorn of context and tone of voice is quite incomprehensible: consider the string of vocables or letters 'He's coming down on Thursday.' Even if this is in English (itself a contextual point), there are indefinitely many senses in which it could be taken: coming from a hilltop, or the North, or university, upon a day of the week or a pet donkey, or is he rebuking someone? Of course, written messages (like this one) can be understood if certain things are taken for granted, though tone of voice and intention are not easily imagined. But our capacity to write messages is distinctively different from our capacity merely to utter them and to be understood in concrete situations. It seems to involve acceptance of a common context, and is easily subverted by changes in those public assumptions (16). How easily do we understand our own notes to ourselves when we have forgotten what they are about?

Such a (relative) ability to understand things in the abstract is connected with an ability, not shown by brain-damaged humans, to perform acts outside their usual context. Such unfortunates can walk up to their rooms and tie their ties, but cannot say how to do it, nor even show what needs to be done (cannot, for example, move their hands *as if* tying a tie). The same incapacity descends on all of us at times: we suddenly discover how much, in normal times, we're carried by our bodies, and cannot achieve the same result by reason.

Some failures of abstraction may be commoner among our non-human kin. We have, after all, been selected for just these abilities, and it is no surprise that even chimpanzees and gorillas do not advance so far. It is surprising for some commentators that they have managed even as much, that they can put a name to things and to themselves. Whether they have yet truly acquired a grammar is a matter still in dispute, but not one, I think, that need concern me now. That they can name things should not be all that surprising. Although it is commonly asserted that 'animals' cannot 'abstract' there is clear counter-evidence at hand. First of all, in the schematic nature of 'releasing mechanisms'. The very fact that pared-down models of predators, rivals, parents can elicit the behaviour appropriate to the concrete entity that is modelled (avoidance, opposition, begging) constitutes the beginning of symbolism as well as the recognition of a common form in many different instances. The forms that beasts recognize may not be the ones that best serve their goals: frogs snap at moving inedibles, not stationary food, and sticklebacks react to 'non-naturalistic red bellies' (35). But, apart from the difficulties already mentioned of disentangling their desires and their beliefs, we certainly cannot conclude that this is sheer automatism. The creatures concerned simply select a different recognition pattern from the one the experimenters use: what we think is much more like a stickleback does not seem so to sticklebacks.

These innate patterns of recognition, this readiness to form and respond to a particular pattern in a medley of swiftly changing shapes, are probably to be found in us as well. We readily respond to cuteness (large head, large eyes, small limbs, engaging clumsiness) even in cartoons (31). More seri-ously, we see circles and other such regular shapes where any strict measurement would reveal quite other forms. We carry our geometry around with us.

A second sort of evidence that beasts can abstract is that laboratory animals (e.g. rats) can be brought to generalize their expectation of reward or punishment, say, from the sight of a horizontal bar to a horizontal row of dots or squares (47). They can form a concept from a limited range of examples which allows them to classify initially dissimilar cases along with the first: they can get the hang of the discrimination that the experimenter wishes to elicit from them. If they can do this much, there seems no great advance in associating an arbitrary sign with all things of this kind. Sarah's ability to handle symbols has recently been confirmed by showing her grasp on analogy: as banana peel is to a banana, so orange peel is to an orange (41). Chimpanzees using Yerkish, a visual code, have demonstrated a similar ability to recognize abstract relationships (85).

Generalizing to a concept of a relationship, such as implication or rejection, is not necessarily more difficult. Creatures who really had no understanding that one act leads to another, and that some acts are quite incompatible, would not last long. Of course, it may be that in the wild most beasts are not confronted by such major problems: their path is mapped for them. When they have sufficient imagination to envisage alternatives they may have problems. Fromm indeed suggests that a chimpanzee, Goliath, torn between bananas and a female on heat, displayed an indecisiveness, an inability to enjoy either one, that would be diagnosed as an obsessional state in human beings (40). He overestimates, maybe, our usual integrity. But it is possible that such apes have seen so far as to understand that there are exclusive alternatives, but have not entered into the kingdom of conceptual thought and argument. If Ameslan is as enthusiastically received by some as some reports suggest, it is not difficult to think that normal evolutionary processes might in the end produce *Pan sapiens*. If we are not special creations, how else did we arrive?

Chapter 4

FREEDOM AND NECESSITY

Desires and inhibitions

A fight between two wolves can be abruptly terminated by the loser's submission. The victor will then stand snarling above the exposed neck of the other, but will not bite. Or rather, does not usually bite (in the presence of the zoologist). He does not simply lose interest and go about some other business, but continues tense and threatening. His desire to seize his rival seems inhibited (64).

This is the sort of case which most readily suggests itself as some sort of analogue of moral conscience, though one (it is reported) much more certain in effect than any qualms we feel. These bars against carrying a behaviour pattern to its logical conclusion need to be stronger in animals more dangerous than men. Doves react to defeat by fleeing: if the loser cannot flee, the victor is not inhibited from pecking the other to death. Men, it is said, have lost their way, because their inhibitions are those of a relatively free-ranging, harmless ape, but their capabilities have been artificially increased by weaponry. Lorenz did not commit himself to saying that men felt no such compunction about butchering their fellows, even with bare hands, but he and his followers do appear to think that it is very difficult for one unarmed human to kill another, that our murderous career only began when we invented clubs.

Two points may be questioned here. In the first place, it is not so difficult for naked humans to kill. We do not have strong claws or piercing teeth; we do have arms and hands and feet, and (equally important) we are vulnerable. It does not need a club to kill. In the second place, perhaps we are quite strongly inhibited against doing that. When ethologists enquire why no other animal engages in mass murder, and conclude that our inhibitory mechanisms do not work as well as theirs, we may justly reply that no other animals have the technical and political capacity to kill in millions. If they had, we cannot be sure that they would not.

A case is reported from the Gombe chimpanzees of a chimpanzee's hugging a young baboon which she is gnawing at. As the baboon struggles and cries the ape responds by panic-stricken hugging, and goes on eating (102). It is a reasonable conclusion that the similarity of young baboon to young chimpanzee is strong enough to cause ambivalent feelings in the ape, but not strong enough to stop the killing. A mother and daughter pair are reported not to be inhibited even from catching and eating baby chimpanzees of their own group (55). Strange chimpanzees may be game, though some ambivalence is shown in the eating of them (11, 32). Considering how little time we have had to consider beasts in their natural setting it would be very rash to claim that their inhibitions are all that much stronger than ours.

Furthermore, we should not suppose that the bar on killing, where it exists, prevents all killing of all conspecifics. That is not, in general, its scope. Strange rats are torn to pieces. It is familiars, and to some extent (but not all that much) children, that we are inhibited about killing. It is very easy not to be inhibited about strangers, particularly if they look or smell or sound unlike ourselves. We are not unlike animals here. These barriers against those of other lands and ways are, after all, the beginnings of new species. So far from being less inhibited about killing our conspecifics than other animals are, it may turn out that we are more so (but that, of course, does not say much).

Are the inhibitions that wolves feel anything like moral ones? Whether the inhibitions, the squeamishness, we ourselves feel are strictly moral ones, is a question I shall tackle later. What of wolves?

Or what of dance flies? Male dance flies have, in some species, progressed from offering a placatory insect to the female (thereby avoiding the supreme sacrifice) to offering merely a silk balloon with no meal inside at all: an example also of ritualized action as the beginning of communication (64). Is the female thereby inhibited from eating the male, as a male mammal is inhibited from attacking a female by her 'submission'? Is the dance fly at all like a moral being?

About such insects we should really be agnostic, but it seems more plausible to say that the male is only giving her something to occupy her, that the only conflict in her, if there is one at all, is between two desires. That is not quite enough to make the analogy with moral inhibition. The conflict of two desires, to have one's cake and eat it too, is a contingent matter: if there were two cakes all would be well. The moralizing interpretation of wolf behaviour requires that the wolf wants to kill his rival, but is averse to doing so. This is that odd relationship with oneself that Plato analyzed in terms of a divided soul: if one is angry with oneself, if one is averse to the very thing to which one is attracted (and averse to one's own attraction), then the self that is angry is not identical with the self that is being rebuked. Such emotions as shame and pride are more than ordinary desires (for food or sex or companionship) because they involve attitudes towards one's own impulses, one's own acts.

If the wolf were not inhibited, he would kill his rival. How do we know? How do we tell what desires creatures have (supposing that we do not just postulate them), except by judging what desires they must have to act as they do if they have an accurate grasp of the situation? If we can assume that the wolf believes (would be surprised if things turned out otherwise) that he can kill his rival by slashing open his throat, we must surely conclude from his failure to do so that he doesn't want to. That he continues snarling does not show he wants to kill, but (if anything) that he wants to make clear his mastery, both to his defeated rival and to any other wolf who's watching. Is not the assumption that his desire to kill is inhibited merely a product of the ancient error that wolves must really be murderous beasts – and if they fail to murder, something must be restraining them? How many of us actually want to kill our friends and lovers even when we're angry with them? Why assume that those who do turn killer are doing what we wanted to do but were inhibited from doing?

That the wolf is in any helpful sense morally inhibited is also made doubtful by the absence of social disapproval. The infanticidal chimpanzees are plainly social dangers, and are resisted, but there seems no way of expressing moral outrage (55). Chimpanzees are, of course, a relatively anarchic species, and such kinds as wolves, with more structured societies, may have more scope for social control. At any rate the alpha wolf may defend his subordinates against his own best rival, beta. It is possible that the rules of squabbling are enforced by senior members of society, and internalized by all. Domestic dogs at any rate show some signs of a 'super-ego', shame and appeasement when they've done some wrong. Their susceptibility to such indoctrination is not implausibly related to their ancestry as wolves, embedded in a social structure which requires that individual impulse be constrained. Dominance relationships will concern me later.

The question why we should impute to wolves both a desire to kill and an inhibition, rather than merely reassess our judgement of what they want, is perhaps answerable in terms of the ideal models of Galilean science. We postulate a relatively simple, brutal range of desires (drives, tendencies), and any deviation from what is expected must be explained by an additional circuit. If we assume that moving objects ideally move in a straight line, then any deviation makes us postulate

36

some disruptive force (friction, gravity, magnets or a push). Our calculations work better so. But it may sometimes be better to assume instead that what is done is just what that sort of thing does do, that no additional circuits are needed to explain the event. Such epicycles are, of course, quite possible, and it may be that a neurological basis could be found for the model of desire plus inhibition: if some part of the brain be removed the animal may act out a pattern which would otherwise be suppressed. But it is not clear that such radical interference leaves the organism unmarred in other ways: the whole system has been disrupted.

An alternative to both models so far suggested (that of an inhibition imposed upon a desire, and that of a different desire than we had supposed) might be derived from introspection. If I make to strike a child (or even look as if I might), the child may cower a little (sucks in breath, raises hands, retreats): this is usually enough, not to inhibit a continuing desire, but simply to cause the evaporation of the desire to strike. Perhaps this is how things are for wolves: while fighting, each may be focused on the other as an enemy, to be beaten down and hurt; when one admits defeat, the other is recalled to treating him as a fellow, and the rage is dissipated.

Freedom

Such shifts involve a change of role and relationship, recalling McBride's dictum: 'animals are all like werewolves' (66). This too requires examination. But I must first consider what seems to some the crucial difference between beasts and men, that animals are not free. The victorious wolf, it is said, cannot kill his rival. Human beings, all too obviously, can. Wolves' obedience to a pattern of mercy, whether or not they also experience a desire to do otherwise, is not optional. As such it is no clear analogy with moral sense. A related point is often made in considering the condition of animals in the wild or in captivity: as in Leyhausen's confused remark that 'no free-ranging animal has freedom of movement, i.e. moves as it pleases and at random' (65, p. 99).

Moving at pleasure is not the same as random motion, for what pleases us may be constant. So we could rephrase the claim as this: No free-ranging animal moves at random, or by random whim. There are constant patterns of behaviour which may seem to be, sometimes may be, intelligent adaptation of ways and means to goals (themselves relatively constant, or at least regular; such as food, sex, shelter). Does this constitute unfreedom? Are we free if we act on random impulse, not if we live out definite patterns of behaviour in a relatively predictable way? This equation of freedom with unlimited possibility, with random action, is very ill-founded.

What is it to be free? The question can be raised in politics and metaphysics, and many different answers given. Liberty of spontaneity, technically so called, consists in doing what one wants. To marry the man of one's choice, because one wants to do so, is to do so freely. To be unfree is to be compelled to act against one's wishes (there are standard difficulties here about coercion: am I unfree if, in order to save my life, which I want to save, I betray a secret I do not want to betray?). On this account it turns out that any willing act of mine is free. Others may wonder whether all my wants are wants I want to have (am I brainwashed, hypnotized, or simply ignorant?), or whether I would want to be in the situation that constrains my options: I am free if nothing in my situation stops me doing what I would seriously want to do, or perhaps if nobody does (for is my freedom really limited by physical law for which no one is responsible?).

Such freedom as this is quite compatible with its being impossible for me to want anything but what, in my situation, I do want. My freedom is not limited by my desires and character. Free-ranging animals are entirely free if no one stops them doing what or going where they want to do or go. Of course, even without the interference of human game-wardens, zoo-keepers and the like, such freedom may often be limited for many of the beasts. Only dominant animals get to do entirely what they want: their 'subordinates' may often be constrained, and hence unfree. But it is surely wrong to say that beasts have no experience of freedom merely because they have a relatively limited range of options, or of territory, in the wild. How much they mind about captivity and constraint is another question, which is not made easier to answer by confusing the issue.

Liberty of indifference, on the other hand, requires that one be able, when one acts, to do otherwise than in fact one does. Only if it is really possible for me to do otherwise is the act one for which I am truly responsible. If I do what I want, because I want to, then my act issues from that fact as its cause: whence comes the want? Are not my acts merely stages in a causal sequence that began with the first moment of creation? Or are they random events, lacking all causal continuity with what went before (i.e. there are no natural laws that say 'In every situation S, an entity type E does action A')? If they are random, on the other hand, can I be blamed for them? They do not stem from any feature of my character - how are they mine?

The freedom of being really able to do otherwise was introduced to save the Creator's credit: unless it is really possible for us not to sin, that sin lies at the Creator's door. But there is reason to think that even unbelievers may require the concept. If we abandon any claim to such bizarre liberty, how can we continue to blame or praise people for what they could not help but do? How can we even instruct anyone to do the best he can? Whatever he does is all he can do, both the best and the worst. Something can be salvaged from the ruin by considering consequentialist arguments for blaming, praising and advising people so, but any genuine attempt to live with pure determinism, even determinism slightly weakened by a random element, must involve a radical restructuring of our whole attitude to ourselves and others.

Animal studies will not much advance our understanding of this crux, for it is not a scientific question whether we are 'free' or not. It is not even very clear what this liberty of indifference amounts to. We are heirs, as so often, of disparate traditions: on the one hand, we believe that all events in the physical universe can be understood as the operation of the laws of nature, such that any given state of things issues ineluctably in a given effect (though there will be difficulties about defining the limits of 'a given state of things'). On the other, we suppose ourselves to be subject to a moral law (which includes the rules of scientific accuracy) that requires us to be free agents, at liberty to do and to refrain. We may hope to find a frontier between these provinces, of freedom and necessity, in the behaviour of non-human animals. But the province of necessity seems likely to swallow us all up: human beings are physical mechanisms, their thoughts and desires the product (the by-product?) of neurological and glandular events determined by the laws of physics. We are organisms too complex for such calculations to have much predictive force, and therefore rely on psychological guesswork in our social relationships. But in the end we ought to hope that explanations such as 'He's just feeling mean', 'She's angry, lustful, wants to ride a horse', will be replaced by accurate neurology. Psychological determinism ('We do what we want because we want to') will give way to physical ('We do what we want because the neurological pathways channel energy appropriately').

Unfortunately, it is not only moral calculation that must suffer a sea-change. Epistemology, and science itself, rests on the felt obligation to follow the evidence, to be good scientists and scholars. These too lapse. Determinists cannot in consistency allow that any rule of argument obliges them to believe in determinism. Their advocacy must become rhetorical, designed to convince, not rationally to oblige. The point is not that a determined system could not be determined to 'believe' a truth, but that genuine obligation requires liberty (9). It is in our experience of being obliged, both morally and epistemologically, that we find our freedom, not as a fact to be observed in the phenomena (which can all be described in accordance with some natural laws) but as a postulate to ground our rationality. We are not simply parts of the world. Instead we may decide to understand necessity, not freedom, as the secondary thing. The physical universe is describable, let us suppose, by some relatively simple rules which permit the inference of one state from another. What rules are operative is a consequence of the choices we free spirits make beyond the world: the universe is what results from all the choices of free spirits embodied in a common realm. Our choices here and now are not determined by the physical universe: the physical universe is determined by the choices we make, have made, outside time.

This Kantian picture may seem topsy-turvy to our modern minds. The point is that it cannot be proved or disproved by studying the overt behaviour of animals or men. It is a transcendental doctrine, adopted with good reason even if in error. It is not we phenomenal beings that are free, of course, but our transcendent selves, and that itself creates a problem. My reason for developing the theory here is that such Kantianism alone seems likely to give us reason to think that 'we' are free, in this strong sense, but that the beasts are not. Only beings that can be obliged, and feel themselves obliged, by rules, are free. The wolves' unfreedom lies in this, that they are not obliged, nor do they think themselves obliged, to spare their foes: they are only inclined to spare them.

Obedience to rule and duty is a later topic, so I shall not here enquire how we could know. It is at least worth noticing that by Kant's standards wolves, although not moral beings, may be ordinarily (not absolutely) good. Even if they do not spare their foes because they think they ought, because it is their duty, they may do so out of the goodness of their hearts. Most of us, despite the Kantians, act out our ordinary affections and praise each other for so doing. We love and are compassionate, angry or tolerant. We think ill of those who lack normal affections and concerns. The problem with psychopaths is not so much that they lack a sense of duty (though

40

they may), but that they do not care about other people, and their desires are not extinguished, changed or inhibited by the sight of distress.

Self-awareness and instinct

One last attempt to see what freedom might consist in, without advancing up to Kantian heights: even if we accept that all things are determined, is there not room for something more than liberty of spontaneity? Some creatures do as they please; others are able to inspect what pleases them, to inspect the causes that have led them to this point, and so be moved to change their ways. This change is as determined as anything else, but what it is determined by is, in part, the self-awareness of the agent. We can be free because we can recognize what is determining us. If I am enraged with my son, I can remember that I am more irritable than usual today, and so not act out all my rage on him (71). My understanding of my own condition and the causes that press hard on me releases me to act a little otherwise. The effort of moral education is just this, to help people to remember who they are and where, and not just act out every impulse as it comes.

So what about the wolves? Do they, when their desire evaporates or is inhibited, suddenly remember themselves? Do they, remembering themselves, refrain from acting out their rage and walk away stiff-legged? Can they, or their past, be objects to themselves? If they cannot be, then they are not free in this last sense.

Suppose they are not. What may we learn from them? They act as they do, and refrain from acting when they do, because they are constrained to do so by their innate behaviour patterns - or else, for this point is unclear, by learned behaviour patterns of a kind that they find relatively easy to acquire. Are our difficulties in achieving civil peace the result of a failure of such patterning? The thing is not impossible. Primates, including young human beings, do not find it natural to be house-trained. In this they are in marked contrast with such creatures as cats, who readily acquire the habit. Infants do not instinctively deposit excrement in some convenient place. The differences between human and feline young are presumably related to their evolutionary history. Sphincter control is no great advantage to young primates, who need not fear to foul their nests. Only since we took to settled existence has it greatly mattered, so such control develops late - though it would be an exaggeration to say that it is wholly an artificial virtue: children, after all, do develop it quite suddenly, in the end, with no need of draconian measures to compel the gift.

Could it be that we are similarly slack in developing any control over our tempers, that we continue too readily to beat and kill our foes? Must mercy be an artificial virtue in us, something inculcated, beaten into us by the usual techniques of conditioning? Conscience, for some, is a conditioned reflex (36); likewise the sudden loss of any desire to kill. It is difficult to see what control-experiment could settle this: any child allowed to grow without the constant communication of adult concern and conscientiousness would be so radically disturbed in any case that the 'absence of conscience' would not show that only conditioning produces conscience. It does not seem plausible to me that children reared with beatings for each small offence would end up very moral men: uptight and prone to violence, perhaps. However, if that is our situation, then maybe morals must be beaten into men, even if this has unfortunate effects. If our children will grow up to be psychopathic murderers unless we beat them (or mark each error in some equally unpleasant way), then we do not have much choice.

But why should we suppose this? It is obvious enough that infants are not toilet-trained from birth. Is it obvious that they pay no attention to another's distress, seek always to secure their victories at any cost, and never spare the defeated? Certainly they are somewhat more self-preoccupied than we might wish, continue fights a little beyond the danger point. So much can be expected: young primates do not need to be all that careful about killing people, since they have not the strength. If they had, there would be more dead parents (killed in sudden rage, not long-drawn vengeance). The young of other species may be in similar case: they go on a bit longer than their adults can quite stand, so getting a salutary lesson in the structure of society. But as they grow in strength their capacity to remember wider issues, see creatures with a different eye than that of rage, must also grow. People, I suggest, do not seriously, in their right minds, wish to hurt and kill their fellows. We have better things to do with each other than that.

Then why are wars and murders quite so common? Why is massacring villages such commonplace human behaviour (53)? Because there are ways of turning off our normal humanity (the villagers are heretics or savages or gooks or something not quite human, and our cause is just); because some people, in demand in certain times and places, turn out psychopathic, who can be controlled (if at all) only by the constant threat of punishment; because it pays some stay-at-homes to send their children out to kill and die. What common features there may be in the heredity or early upbringing of psychopaths, whose desire to kill does not evaporate when faced by an appeal to mercy, is a matter for enquiry. It is worth noting that Harlow's motherless, raped monkeys treated their infants as they would have treated rats. The denial of love breeds monsters. Having been raised without social contact, with dummy 'mothers', they lacked all empathy (45).

On this latter view, conscience and the cooling of our anger need not be beaten into children. Given anything approaching a decent environment it will develop. How should it not? Our ancestors have lived in social circles since long before they were human. In the absence of more evidence than has yet been offered us, we must suspect that those who doubt that mercy is a natural virtue have been too much influenced by child-rearing theory of an older sort than Spock. The psychopath is not the natural man, any more than is a man who shits and pisses without thinking where.

Chapter 5

ME AND MINE

Selfhood and language

To be convinced of our transcendental, Kantian freedom we
need to be aware of ourselves as being subject to obligations.
To be liberated from our former ways we need to be aware of
ourselves as having been in them. On some accounts of moral
sense and inhibition we must have an attitude to our own
attitudes, be angry or complacent about our own desires and
acts. We need to be aware of ourselves as objects.

This is very much the awakening from which I began this
treatise: the sudden realization that one has been speaking
prose all one's life, that one is a chauvinist, that all one's acts
have stemmed from Oedipal jealousy. Realizing this we realize
a deeper level of ourselves, a level that may have its own
unconscious motives but at least is free not to continue the old
ways, once they are known. Such awakenings can be observed
in others when they result in changes, blossomings of half-
forgotten seeds, or sudden collapses of a noble virtue. The
realization that there is no cosmic law to make one faithful,
courteous or brave may give us a chance to go against those
rules. But awakenings may not be so abrupt in their effect:
sometimes awakened souls continue knowingly with their past
lives. We cannot always tell what spiritual changes are involved. But of course even such as are, strangely, converted to
the very faith they held before may reveal some alteration, if
not in their plan of life (which now truly is a plan), at least in
their mannerisms or their style of dreaming.

Is such awareness of oneself as an object in the world,
with the corresponding possibility of taking an attitude to, or
changing, what has been, something of which beasts are
capable (20)? The common assumption is that it is not, just as
it is commonly assumed that men are the only animals aware
of their death. It is not easy to imagine observations which
would decide this point, and in most cases we should be
agnostic. We certainly should not conclude, as too many
positivists have done, from the (supposed) scientific undecida-
bility of a question to the scientific ineluctability of one
particular answer. Failure to prove one thing does not prove
the contrary. Sometimes, of course, we must take sides
without sufficient evidence, and should then reckon up which
would be the worse error: to impute self-awareness where

44

none exists, or to deny it where it does. And of course, though we find it difficult to articulate our evidence, we may trust our intuitive judgement that men are sometimes self-aware and tapeworms aren't: what use would self-awareness be to them? Those who rely upon such intuitions should take care not to overstate their case: when Reynolds (81, p. 189) claims that there is *every* reason to doubt that animals envisage how they are seen by others (a point related, as I shall argue, to the thoughts of self and death), he conspicuously fails to mention even one of these innumerable reasons.

What might they be? Lucy, one of the Ameslan apes, was reared within a human household. In her infancy her self-styled 'father' was able to cajole and bully her into eating meat; she later ceased to be susceptible to this, ceased living for his approval (92). We cannot tell, at least from Temerlin's account, what went on in her mind, but one possibility is just that sort of self-realizing moment. This is how human children suddenly discover that they are being teased or tricked. To say that this is anthropomorphic is to beg the question: what reason have we to think that it is as men that we are self-aware, and not as primates, mammals, amniota (a biologocal taxon including reptiles, birds and mammals), animals? Merely that strange conceit which requires the things we value most to be things unique to men?

Our first guess might be that beasts do not talk, and lacking language cannot have a concept of themselves. Paradoxically, Cartesians are not well equipped to make this point, simply because they think that we can form a concept of our self, and an assurance of our self's existence, independently of any public language. Descartes' reason for thinking that beasts did not think was that they did not talk (and that to suppose them thinking things would impose too great a moral burden on us), but he did not reckon that thought was only possible in a public language. If that is so then the Cartesian ego cannot get started, cannot speak of 'I' even to itself. One can refer to oneself only in terms whose definition and criteria anyone could learn. I can refer to myself only if I can know when others make the selfsame reference, only if I can translate 'You're standing on my toe' (your words) into 'I am standing on yours' (my words). I can only think about myself if I can talk about myself, and I can only do the latter if I can understand it when you talk about yourself (or me). Since animals do not share a language capable of such references and transmutations, they cannot think about themselves, have no self-awareness.

If having a concept of the self consists in being able to

use language in this way, then those that cannot talk have no concept of self. Ameslan apes do appear to be able to handle this much of language, to recognize pictures of themselves and to report what they want and are doing. A full grasp of self, involving the grammatical transformations mentioned above, is less clearly established. It seems difficult for students to consider the situation calmly enough to be reliable witnesses: some are enthusiasts for talking chimpanzees, others just as ideologically convinced that all who report such conversations must be quite misled (62, 87, 93). Fascinating as they are, I have to conclude that the Ameslan apes are best left out of the picture, for the moment.

The real question is rather: What is necessary if one is to acquire such a linguistic ability? If I can learn a word for something, I must first have grasped that thing as something nameable, whether it be a tree, a cat, a word. How do infants know what is being talked about if they have no concept of the self before they have learnt the language? How do they learn the language if they do not know what it's all about? How plausible is the idealist claim that being a certain thing simply consists in regularly, properly being called that thing within a given speech community? There is a sense in which blood's being red simply consists in its being called 'red' by competent English speakers: if we all agreed to call it 'rouge' it would be rouge. But in another sense its being red is just a fact, unchanged whatever we call it: it is the sort of thing that *we* call 'red'. Infants do not need to talk to be able to recognize sameness of colour or of shape, identity of person or cause of woe. They recognize, and show in what they do that they recognize, all sorts of things to which they cannot give a name: they classify things. Why should they not be able to distinguish self and other, self and world, or acknowledge things or acts as theirs, before they find the words to speak of this? They will only understand, and learn to use, the words if they can see what is being talked about.

What are being talked about are persons, of course, not Cartesian selves: reidentifiable psychophysical organisms that act and co-operate and commit themselves. To that extent the concept that infants must have, and beasts surely may have, is not of a self separable from all public involvement, but of a being in the world. Those who attempt the Cartesian *epoche* (disconnecting our primitive belief that the world outside us really exists) will find that in eliminating world, and friends and body they have also lost themselves. Few philosophers now think that the grounds of all conviction lie in our certainty of self.

If beasts have no conception of Cartesian selves that is to their credit. I can see no reason why they, and human infants, may not have a pre-verbal concept of the beings that they are, distinct from others and from the environment, and having policies that are all their own (however short-term). Without such concepts I cannot see that human infants could acquire a language. Having a concept and being able to consider it are different things. I may have the concept of redness long before I can talk about redness or relate it to a general theory of perception. I may use the concept of moral accountability long before I can consider what such a thing might be. The Socratic enterprise was precisely an attempt to make people seek to analyse and understand the very concepts that they used unthinkingly. Thus Socrates characteristically argued that be-cause all definitions of, say, justice that his victims gave conflicted with their intuitions of what act was just, they therefore did not know what justice was - but in another sense they knew quite well what acts were just, and Socrates counted on that knowledge to disprove the definitions. The normal state of most of us is this: to know quite well what we do not understand. Beasts, maybe, are in no worse state than we.

The self in action

Analysis of freedom and morality suggests that selves are beings obliged by rules, with more capacities than they dis-play, and able to inspect their own desires. To have such a concept one must recognize other beings in the world, distin-guish what is self and what is not-self, and lay claim to pasts and futures of the single being one is. To have a concept of the self is, in part at least, to do these things: to show awareness of the world as being more than one's immediate perception of it, to recognize other beings as being the same as some past acquaintances, to admit responsibility for past action and to intend some future.

Before attempting the vexed question whether beasts do these things, it is worth remembering that not every thinker thinks these things worth doing. Some have held that our goal should be to advance again to an unselfconscious involvement in the world and action, that the necessary detour through self-awareness is, in the end, delusory. Before enlightenment, cutting wood and drawing water; after enlightenment, cutting wood and drawing water. It may turn out in the end that our particular form of consciousness is only a particular way of life. While we ordinarily think that the moral revolution which disallowed the punishment of any other than the single guilty person, not that person's family, was an acknowledgement that the individual was the real thing, it may be instead that 'the individual' was created then, that there is as much good reason to consider momentary selves or families as real bearers of responsibility. Selfhood may be a social construct after all.

But first to consider animals. Do some distinguish between self and world? Do they treat their own limbs as they would treat just any other object? On some occasions, yes: rats may carry their own tails when, if they had the chance, they would carry cubs or nest material. Cats pounce on their tails in play. But these acts, exactly, are in play, are substitutes for other acts. Human beings too manipulate their own limbs, bodies, when there's nothing else to do: we do not conclude of masturbators that they can't distinguish self and world, nor that they show stupidity by such mistakes. In general, beasts do treat their own selves differently from objects in the world: a necessary, not sufficient part of the distinction between self and world. It is not sufficient simply because such a difference of treatment is required for any living organism, whether or not it is mediated even by differences of pain and pleasure: it must not digest itself, nor prepare antibodies against its own organs.

What other important distinction between self and world is to be made? Beings who did not so distinguish would observe a constant shift of shapes and colours, that vanish and reform. They would not suppose that anything existed unperceived by them; they would not return to places, nor be reacquainted with old friends. To realize that things continue unperceived by us, that the selfsame thing may reappear, that things do keep their places, is to take one huge step away from unthinking solipsism (16). Even for us, for adult humans, this can be a discovery whose implications we had not understood: one's spouse exists, and London, and even now both beasts and men are somewhere dying slowly. Such additional discoveries of what exists may be beyond most animals. But at least they show a grasp of how they move through a relatively stable world; they develop cognitive maps, in which they track their own progress through the world. They can recognize the same thing back again, and relocate both things and places. Once again, they had better be able to. Few animals wander quite at random through the world, uncaring where they are. Some cases of relocation may be explained more simply: salmon, say, may simply climb the gradient of their home-river's scent. Other creatures, particularly migrants, may recognize landmarks. Hunting species, such as wolves and men, must cover

large ranges, and have correspondingly well-developed cognitive maps. Not to be aware of how the world is itself, not
just how it appears to us at any given time, would be a
disadvantage. Accordingly, we may assume that most mobile
creatures do distinguish, in practice, between the world
through which they move and their own selves that move
through it.

That beasts can reidentify places and things is, in a sense,
enough to show that they can identify other beasts. But
something more is required than that. The point involved in a
grasp of selfhood is that it is a social concept: to be aware of
myself as myself is to enter into a social nexus where things
and deeds are attributed to me by others, and I attribute
things and deeds to them. I must recognize them as selves, and
be recognized by them. This is not so in every social species.
Rats appear to treat all other rats (at least of their own pack)
as universalizing moralists would wish: with superb impartiali-
ty. They do not seem to recognize each other as individuals at
all, nor to recognize any special bonds. Even in species where
more special ties exist we cannot always say that individuals
are recognized as such: storks form breeding pairs, but more
(it seems) because the male and female territories coincide
than for any special quasi-marital bond. But where individuals
do recognize each other, as mates or clan-mates or as 'the
irritable male who can still outface me when he wishes', then
we have good reason to think that the animals have at least
the beginnings of a concept of their own identity. The societies of the higher primates, in particular, are clearly societies
of individuals, mutually recognized as such. Recent work with
vervet monkeys shows that mothers not only identify their own
child's cry, but also recognize whose child (other than their
own) is crying - they look towards the mother who is being
called (15).

Such recognition may go along with a recognition of the
other's claim on goods. When a chimpanzee begs for a share of
meat, rather than simply grabbing it, there is implicit acknowledgement of the other's right to dispose of that meat. This
may, of course, be simply that a straight demand might lead to
a fight more serious than the meat is worth, but the behaviour
may still be significant (55).

For there is one notorious way in which beasts lay claim
on goods, and seemingly respect the claims of others: namely,
territorial behaviour. Some popular accounts of this have made
it seem that all men are doomed to selfish hoarding of some
land, some good, some property. In fact there is reason to
doubt that men are very territorial animals (80). Neither

chimpanzees nor gorillas maintain strict territorial defences between individuals or betwen groups; nor do hunter-gatherers (this is not to say that they welcome strangers, nor that they are ideally peaceable) (32). Territory, for human beings, looks much more like a social development to suit the rise of agriculture and the nation-state. But my point here is not the right-wing ideology of popular ethologists, but territory as it exists in beasts.

Strictly, 'territory' is a blanket term (91). It has been used to mean the 'home range' (the area usually or chiefly covered by the animal) as well as the area defended by the animal (which is the better and more helpful use). Individuals have territories, and so do pairs and groups of animals. Much territorial analysis has had to do with birds, who maintain various kinds. The scrub jay defends a small range; the pinon jay defends only a nesting area within a large range; Steller's jays defend their nests within a large shared range which they occupy hierarchically; Mexican jays are commune dwellers, co-operating in the rearing of their young (10). Some birds defend the area in which they display for mates, and male birds of some kinds congregate in leks (display areas where each male defends a symbolic piece of land, or sapling); others defend their nesting area; others again a larger area where they get their food. Sea-birds, for obvious reasons, do not have territorial ambitions over the sea; land-birds, where food is scarce, attempt to hold as much land as will support them and their chicks. Since birds can fly, their territories have clear boundaries. Mammals with territories do not defend their frontiers, but their chosen paths (60). My suspicion is that much of what passes for territorialism in mammals is no more than group solidarity, but there is no need to decide the matter here.

My point is that individual animals may lay claim upon a particular stretch of ground and defend it against (chiefly male) rivals. More importantly, they seem to acknowledge rights of possession: that is, intruding males are readily discouraged, fight less well, than the possessor. Even butter-flies seem to give the current occupant of a patch of light the moral edge over an intruder. If this tendency is combined (as I do not suggest it is in butterflies) with a capacity to recognize other individuals, we have a further element in the genuine grasp of self as an owner among other owners. It is in respecting others' claims that I display my demands upon the world as being *claims*. I can only claim a right to anything if I will cede that selfsame right to other creatures similarly placed. Territorial division of the land provides that possibility.

But even if I can recognize other individuals, and expect to be recognized by them; even if I can be aware of where I am within a stable world; even if I lay claims to possess some areas of the world, do I have a concept of myself? Do I acknowledge my past acts and plan my futures? Not all human, even adult, beings do: most of us find it difficult at times to connect the pasts we know we had with what we now experience ourselves to be. Can I really have thought that, felt that, dressed like that? How could that be I? Our memories are sometimes more like diaries from an older world than like our own accumulated history. Turning to the future, few of us consistently plan our long-term goals. Even if we take on duties that can be expected to absorb us for many years it is more because that is how society is arranged than because we feel it natural so to do. None the less, someone who had only a very limited temporal gaze would not have any very strong concept of self.

The most striking acknowledgement of past action by a non-human is probably that of an Ameslan gorilla, Koko, who is reported (*New Scientist*, 30 June 1977) to have expressed regret for having bitten her teacher three days previously, saying that she was cross at the time but did not remember why (it is not alleged that she expressed these things in the form of grammatical sentences). Little can be built on this by itself, but it is not wholly implausible. Even without Ameslan, Mrs Hoyt's gorilla, Toto, allegedly expressed regret at having broken Mrs Hoyt's wrists, or at any rate at her wrists' being broken (79). Holding grudges against cheaters, and feeling compunction at one's own past cheating, can be given some evolutionary function (97). Such feelings must be the natural roots of any full-scale sense of self: we first feel guilt or indignation or gratitude for favours past or pride at what 'we' have done, and from these elements acquire the concept that it was indeed this creature who did that. In fact, thinking of such identity may amount to little more than just this readiness to praise and blame. If this account is true, then our feelings of corporate pride or guilt may not be so absurd: another culture might build up from these a concept of the continuing people, and be as fierce in its defence as we are for our precious selves.

Planning for the future has often been taken as the crucial step. Creatures who respond simply to a present stimulus, preferring one way to another, cannot accept imme-

diately less favourable conditions in the expectation of even
tual success (34). To avoid the obvious problems such short-
sightedness creates, relatively lengthy behavioural sequences
may evolve: in stereotyped situations animals simply get on
with the sequence for which they have been prompted, not
noticing immediate disvalues. Unsurprisingly, animals (including us) put up with things that they would otherwise find
seriously distressing when they are engaged in important
activities (hunting, escaping, mating etc.). The more certain it
is that creatures will embark upon such routines on cue, the
more stereotyped the way in which they perform them, the
less we are inclined to think that this involves any genuine
planning or foresight. But the distinction between this and
'globally maximizing behaviour' of a purposive sort is not
entirely clear. Squirrels are able to go away from something
they desire in order to get round to it: to do so requires that
they accept an immediate disvalue in order that a 'future self'
gain the goal. Of course it is because they are used to such
situations, are evolved to fit them, that they can do this; and
of course the future self they benefit is not a very distant one.
But it is not a wholly automatic, unthinking reflex: they must
trace their path with care. The macaques who toss wheat and
sand into the sea in order to retrieve the wheat are not
engaged in stereotyped behaviour, but accepting a cultural
revolution, initiated by a macaque genius (a young female).
Animals that live in a changing environment cannot rely
simply on stereotyped behaviour: they must take account of
changes, learn from them.

Long-term programmes are not easily detected in our
non-human kin. To that extent they cannot be said to have any
strong concept of self. But we should not conclude that the
acquisition of this strong concept is what marks us off as
human. It is a constant theme in religion, after all, that we
should not plan too far ahead, and our hunter-gatherer ancestors almost certainly did not. Planning for the future is not a
pastime that pays many dividends for hunter-gatherers, who
rely instead upon their knowledge of their own environment,
which can be trusted to provide, if not security for all, at least
sufficient for most usual wants (83). It is only with the growth
of agriculture, and the need to conserve seed to plant for
another season, that global prudence became necessary.
Whether our ancestors were forced to it by their imprudent
overuse of the Pleistocene fauna, or whether they simply
slipped into increased reliance on the herbs the women (probably) were cultivating, we cannot know. Judging from the
attitudes of our contemporary hunter-gatherers, it seems

likely that whereas mercy is a natural virtue, prudence is an artificial one (50) (I owe this insight to my friend Flint Schier). We might conclude the same from our own behaviour: we certainly look likely to repeat the error of our Pleistocene ancestors in over-exploiting the resources that we need, in the hope of an immediate advantage.

Death

One aspect of the sense of self remains: the expectation and imagination of our deaths. Those who can conceive of the world's existence over and above their own perceptions of it, of things and friends going on without them, have the necessary basis for such a sense. That I will have an end is a discovery made by seeing that I am like others who have an end. To recognize myself in a mirror and in any conspecific (8,67) is to realize that we are all subject to the same destiny, that I am not as special as, unthinkingly, I thought.

Beasts flee situations in which they would be, might be, killed, and they may seek to protect their young against predators. Consider a Patas monkey (male) pursuing a jackal with an infant in her jaws (76). Primate mothers may carry their dead young around with them, displaying great distress that the young no longer respond. Lionesses are more likely to eat dead cubs. Elephants, bizarrely (but the practice is well attested), bury dead bodies (27). No one, to my knowledge, has yet worked out any evolutionary explanation of this. The fears and the concerns of beasts do not demonstrate that they fear or recognize death as the irrevocable end of their or others' lives. It is the situations that might kill which they fear or fight against: it does no good to fear sudden death, since we cannot guard against it. We need not think that they, or we, avoid danger so as to avoid death: we avoid danger, and that does, very often, avoid death. Only creatures who have invested emotional energy in the fulfilment of plans, or the welfare of friends, or who are metaphysically appalled by the thought of their own absence from the world, are in a position to fear death as such. Not that all those who are concerned for friends or for their long-term plans must fear death: we are not indispensable to these, and our own deaths may sometimes help our friends, our plans. Not all our deaths are equally abhorrent. A young mother's death is tragedy; a centenarian's is not - unless we're moved to think that particular life wasted. Such assessments and obituaries mark our knowledge that death is a rite of passage, of a living person to a ghost, an ancestor. How beasts feel about their dead we do not know.

For us, the realization of our coming death may be the spur to an awakened life; our appreciation of ourselves as objects in the world may be the moment when we realize we die. But those who have not realized this are not wholly lacking in a sense of self. Likely enough, it is parenthood which drives the message home, in worry for one's child. Less settled animals, maybe, need less reminder of impermanence, and find their contentment in more manageable ways. If so, they do not mark themselves off quite as much as we do.

Selfhood, in its strongest form, comes into the world as part of a social tradition of treating each individual as a separate and innately valuable entity. Not every human tradition has inculcated these values, but even traditions which do not may have to accommodate the sudden wakening that comes when we see ourselves as others see us, and do not like the sight. Mavericks may be the first individuals, the first to have to wonder what to do, the first not to be content with becoming a ghost in a continuing tradition. If there are maverick beasts, who knows?

Chapter 6

ALTRUISM

Altruism and the selfish gene

Creatures that have no conception of themselves as beings in the world, surrounded by other beings with whom they have social relationships, cannot be either selfish or unselfish. They may do things which benefit themselves or which benefit others, but their motive in so doing cannot be the good of any separate being in the world. It is therefore ridiculous to say that the elephant seal displays an egoistical concentration on preventing the loss of his harem at whatever cost to the pups he rolls upon (2), unless it is seriously supposed that the seal has conceived of himself as being one self among others (which he may have). All that can be said of creatures without this concept is that they are more or less distressed by events. There seems no *a priori* reason to insist that they will always be more upset by what happens to their own bodies than by what happens elsewhere in their perceptual frames: perhaps certain sights are more distressful than certain immediate aches and pains, so that the creature would move away from such a sight even if it thereby moved into a more obvious pain.

Once creatures do have some sense of their own identity through time, their standings *vis-à-vis* others of their kind, it becomes possible for them to differentiate things that are bad for them and what is bad for others. I only say that it is possible, and therefore possible that they be egoists or altruists. Ants who advance into a fire, with the result that in the end their fellows may be able to cross upon a bridge of dead bodies, are only with difficulty imagined as performing an act of heroic self-sacrifice. Surely (we think) they did not intend that consequence, did not reason that this was the optimal solution to their corporate problem, have no conception of their own purposes and selves through time. We confirm ourselves in this by the suspicion that if ants were truly rational and courageous creatures at least some of them would come to the opposite conclusion, and either hang back or quietly desert or go another way.

We recall also that human animals cope with such circumstances, as in war, precisely by submerging their reasoning faculties, even their sense of separate selfhood. How else could a brigade continue marching while being bombed? A balance of fears would, maybe, keep them steady, but if they really were operating as rational individuals they would surely (most of them) desert. We forget ourselves quite easily: how many motorists have suddenly woken from a dream of driving along a motorway to find out that they were? And not all of them have shown great incompetence. Such military or motor-way self-forgetfulness may be the nearest we can get to the consciousness of a creature for whom the self has never been an option. But we may still be wrong: if bees can converse, are we quite sure that ants do not do the same? Easy as it is to repeat the notion that the hives or nests of social insects are more like a single body than a human state, the motions of the separate insects governed by the chemicals released by the queen and not by genuine communication (of an intentional sort), are we perhaps misled?

Still, the probability is that purely automatic patterns of behaviour, selected over many million years, are enough to account for the observed events. Given the particular details of insect reproduction such societies are easier to reach (104) (though recent studies of the naked mole-rat show that these details are not necessary for 'eusociality' to develop (51)). It happens that an individual's nieces will, on average, be more like her than her own children would: an aunt who encourages the production of such nieces will be encouraging, on average, her own reduplication more successfully than if she invested in offspring of her own. It therefore 'pays' the insects to be sterile workers, and exploit a sister as a brood queen: 'pays', that is, in the confusing terminology of genetic theory. Accordingly, as long as one's sister goes on breeding well it does not matter if one lives or dies. Such insects need less investment of emotional energy in their own individual survi-val than do creatures who must live if they are to breed. Accordingly, ants are not courageous: they simply have no need to care about their own individual well-being.

What can we say of creatures more like us, of amniota, and of mammals, and of primates? Do they display altruistic or self-sacrificial behaviour? Many biological texts will now insist that no one, human or non-human, can be 'really' altruistic, and a good deal of popular nonsense has been talked. Biologists have not always made it clear that their account of 'altruism' is radically unlike the common notion. Altruistic behaviour is defined, by biologists, in terms of its consequen-ces (not, as it ordinarily is, in terms of the agent's motives) (75), and the consequence singled out as crucial is an overall diminution of the agent's genetic fitness. That is, behaviour is altruistic ('really altruistic') if it diminishes the likelihood that there will be representatives of the agent's genetic type (with particular reference to the hereditary traits that lead to the behaviour in question) in the next generation. If I am genuinely altruistic I am diminishing the chances of there being genuine altruists in the next generation. It is hardly surprising that behaviour so defined is rare: if it were not it soon would be (24).

Much behaviour that would ordinarily be thought altruistic, as displaying a concern for the good of another creature even at some cost to oneself, is ruled out of court as not being 'genuine' altruism: parental care is not altruistic; neither is concern for siblings, cousins or for those who might return some profit to the agent (whether or not that is the agent's motive). Only concern for very distant, useless relatives is genuinely altruistic, as it would genuinely increase their genetic fitness above the agent's own – and such behaviour is self-eliminating over evolutionary time (97). Accordingly, nobody really cares about Kampuchea (except Kampucheans).

This cynical conclusion – of great comfort to those of us who do not wish to care – that such unrealistic do-gooders who say we ought to care will be eliminated from the species by their own endeavours, has been backed up by all the customary arguments of egoists. If I seek some goal it must be that I think well of it, and so consider it a good for me. If I sacrifice myself for a friend it must be that I wanted something from the act, and only the detail of that want distinguishes me from the 'selfish' person who betrays a friend for gain. On this view we can do nothing but what satisfies our desires, nothing but use each other for our private profit, even if we sometimes fail to secure the expected gain.

In fact it should be obvious that biological argument disposes quite as readily of egoism. 'Genuine' egoists prefer their own individual advantage at whatever cost to their genetic fitness. Or rather, if we adopt the consequentialist account so favoured by biologists: 'genuine' egoists are those whose acts reduce their own genetic fitness and increase their own good (survival, say, or luxury). Accordingly, there are no genuine egoists (or if by chance there are, there won't be soon). Only the biologists' equation of 'advantage' and 'genetic fitness' obscures this point. A concern for one's own good is, as I hope I have shown, a sophisticated attitude. What counts as good for oneself is determined by one's needs and wants, which may include companionship and happy friends. Nothing in biological theory, when correctly stated, precludes the possibility that I would rather that some other creature were content than that I gain some lesser good: I do not seek their good merely as a means to my own happiness – my happiness consists in part in their achieving good (71).

The evolutionary aspects of our lives are none the less worth considering. What the arguments actually suggest is that we have the desires and habits that we do because either they, or else some other feature which has predisposed us to acquire those desires and habits, were in the past such as to lead our ancestors to act in such a way that (in their situation) they had more descendants than those creatures who acted otherwise. Or rather (for evolution is not finished yet) they behaved in ways that did not instantly eliminate their genetic heritage. Desires and habits that we share with all mankind, or all of a particular sub-group of men, are likely to have been adaptive (once), or are (at any rate) not very ill-adaptive side-effects of other features of a more adaptive kind.

The evolutionary paradigm is generally accepted as it refers to our morphology: Caucasians have light skin because it pays them to get all the vitamin D from sunlight that they can; negroes may have sickle-cell anaemia because the hetero-zygotic form of that gene-structure gives an immunity against malaria. Humanistic thinkers have been less willing to accept the moral when it is applied to behaviour. But it seems quite clear that behavioural patterns can be inherited as well as morphological, and are indeed equally secure criteria for species-membership. Human beings doubtless have rather few stereotyped sequences of behaviour, such as start on cue and continue with little attention to the situation. The same is true of most higher mammals. It does not follow that none of their behaviour is species-specific. To name the most obvious: language-learning is a thing that humans do, with enormous speed and against all odds. It may well be that our ancestors could talk before they had developed large brains or intelligent foresight. We are also exceptionally (even if not uniquely) conscious of how others think of us – a fact that has more to do with our troubled history than our supposed freedom from inhibition. Is our altruism of a different order from that of other animals, and if so, why?

Animal altruism

What costly concern for others do other animals show? If a mother bird diverts predators from her brood she runs a risk, but perhaps not one that she perceives as very great. Such behaviour is simply 'what one does', and there is no need to

Altruism

think that she calculates the odds. Evolution has, as it were,
done that for her: mothers who distract predators may some
times get caught themselves (and their brood perish), but in
general, in the situation that has obtained over evolutionary
time, they leave more offspring (probably with that disposition) than those who do not. It 'pays'. Even if she fights to the
death rather than flee, does she know what she is doing? She
does defend something when without that need she probably
could escape, even if she has no picture of her own death to
disturb her. But parents that desert their young too readily
leave no descendants (unless they leave so many that the death
of most makes little difference in the end). Parental altruism
poses no real problem to the evolutionary biologist. It does to
the comparative psychologist - how do we tell what the beast
in question thinks of what she's doing? Despite the more
careless statements of biologists she is certainly not working
to maximize the probability that her genes will be represented
in the next generation. That may be the effect of what she
does: it cannot be her intention, unless she grasps the nature
of population genetics and games theory. But can she be
concerned for another's good?

If monkeys prefer to go hungry rather than press a button
which will give them food but also inflict an electric shock
upon a monkey they can see, is that because they wish the
victim well or because sights like that put them off their
food? If rats will work to save their conspecifics from distress,
is that because they wish them well or because they do not
like the squeaks? Oddly, some experimenters (57) concluded
that rats were not 'real altruists' because they did not work to
stop the recorded squeaks of rats - a fact at least as
convincingly accounted for by supposing that they *were* altruists, and that they did not mind the squeaks but did mind the
perceived fact of suffering. We can distinguish, amongst
ourselves, between a sentimentalism that is hurt by the
thought or sight of others' pain (and reacts by putting it out of
sight or mind) and a genuine concern for others. When Tris-
tram Shandy's Uncle Toby wishes he had not learnt about a
particularly distressing case that, now he knows, he feels
obliged to alleviate, he speaks for us all (sometimes). But of
course the genuine altruist would want to know about such
cases so that he could alleviate them. We can realize that
others exist where we do not, can distinguish between what
they are in themselves and what they are to us. That, maybe,
is our first exclusion, when we realize that our parents have
relationships with each other and with others that do not

59

involve us. Only when we have realized this are we in any position to consider what they need apart from what we need in them. How are non-human animals placed?

Our own escape from infantile and adolescent solipsism is so difficult, and our tendency to relapse so great, that we are inclined to think that other animals do not make this step at all. Everything we escape from and relapse into tends to be equated with mere animal existence. But this need not be the most natural interpretation of behaviour in a social species where individuals are recognized and there are the elements of self-awareness. The Gombe chimpanzees mostly treated one of their number who had contracted polio with hostility and contempt: so much so that Jane Goodall found herself strongly disliking them (58). In this they were like most of us, who find disablement and disease personally repugnant and hate the victims for the unease they cause. One chimpanzee, however, whom Goodall supposed the victim's brother, seemingly transcended the dislike, and tended the sufferer. This may not have involved a strong awareness of the other's being, but at least it differed in technique from the behaviour of those who seek to end the pangs of their own hearts by staying away from the sight. All animals that take account of how their fellows are behaving, and incorporate them into their cognitive maps (of spatial position and hierarchical order), have the chance to work for the good of their fellows or themselves.

Why should they work for the good of others? The question assumes, what evolutionary thought should have disproved, that working for one's own good is more natural. Political theorists regularly assume that social order must be built on selfish men, that men would never accept a set of laws that did not work to their own advantage. This is in fact a thoroughly unnatural notion. The moral revolution that insisted, in the words of Jeremiah, that 'a man shall die for his own wrong-doing; the man who eats sour grapes shall have his own teeth set on edge', was doubtless just: but it is surely obvious that most of us would be far more readily deterred from crime by a threat to 'punish' our children (or any other dear to us) than we are by threats to our own well-being. This may not be true of psychopaths, to whom none (not even their own future selves) are dear, but not all men are psychopathic. If evolutionary argument is taken seriously we must ask what sort of things animals (including us) are likely to care about? The answer is that they will probably care about those things that enticed their ancestors to act in such ways that they at last were born. Long-term, prudential foresight, I have suggested, is a relatively late development still ill-grounded in our heredity; concern for self rests on the fact that animals survive in health, at least long enough to produce and rear children, a little more often if they take some care. In any sexual species, not reproducing by parthenogenesis, that also requires that we be ready to co-operate with others, that we like their company (even if not all the time). In the sort of social groups that primates inhabit we must be concerned for the welfare of our clan-mates, not merely what they can do for 'us'. We do not fear death and distress for our own selves so much as individualists have theorized. We care for those things that have served the commons. Such cares precede the use of reason. In Lorenz's words: 'Our prehuman ancestor was indubitably as true a friend to his friend as a chimpanzee or a dog, as tender and solicitous to the young of his community, and as self-sacrificing in its defence, aeons before he developed conceptual thought and became aware of the consequences of his actions' (64, p. 212). Such altruism and self-sacrifice (with all appropriate caveats about the way animals themselves think) are not universalized, not even to all members of the species. The hunting dogs who are touchingly concerned for their cubs, letting them eat first or else regurgitating food for them and for the dogs who are left to guard them while the hunt's away, feel no compunction about dragging down their prey (less, even, than do human hunters). The rats who, without individual recognition, busy themselves in their own packs will tear strange rats to pieces (strange in smell, that is). Animals do not experience any overriding duty to ensure the survival of the stock, still less the species, to which they belong. That biologists have attempted to impose such a duty on us as that from which all other duties flow testifies more to their humanistic conditioning than to any natural impulses or moral intuitions. We have the desires we do in part because the having of them has developed our stock: it does not follow that we desire or ought to desire the survival of our kind. We do desire the survival and the welfare of our family, our friends: for this we are prepared to work and suffer.

Games theory and war

And that is our problem. Games theory, which is now in vogue among population geneticists as a way of determining what behavioural patterns are likeliest to survive in what situations, has also been of use in political philosophy. The simplest such game is Prisoner's Dilemma. Suppose two men are captured by the police. The police can prove that they have committed a minor offence for which they can expect one year apiece in

Altruism

jail, but also (justifiably) suspect a more serious crime, which they cannot prove against their prisoners. Accordingly they tell the prisoners (separately) that if one confesses he will go free, and the other will get twenty years; if both confess, each will get a reduced sentence of ten years; if neither confesses, each will get sent down for the minor offence, for one year. Each prisoner then calculates as follows: if my colleague is confessing, I had better do the same (or I'll get twenty years); if he is not confessing, I better had (or I'll get one year in jail instead of walking free) - I'd better confess. Since both reason thus, and both confess, they both get ten years in jail when, by silence, they might only have got one.

This example is enough to show that simple egoism may get the wrong result (wrong even by egoistic standards). Solutions fall roughly into three kinds: either we postulate a Mr Big who will punish any confession far more toughly than the police could dare; or we assume that the prisoners actually care for each other, to the point of total trust or total acceptance ('he'll not betray me, and even if he does I'll not betray him'); a third possibility is that the prisoners expect to play the same game indefinitely many times, and so wish to earn a good reputation (but the reasoning is unstable). These solutions correspond to the differing political models of an authoritarian State or a common concern amongst all citizens, unenforced by law. For of course this dilemma corresponds to many of our corporate problems: if others use private transport, I must too; if others don't, I may as well - and so our cities choke. If others seek more pay, I must too; if others don't, I may - and so inflation continues. If others cheat their employers, why may not I? if they don't, I may - and so our businesses collapse. Within the small groups for which our kind, it seems, evolved, such egoism is not troubling (much): we can feel concern for each other well beyond the point of rational 'self-interest', and so we prosper too. The wider unions of the nation-state and of industrial society surpass at times our gift for genuine concern, and are upset not by merely selfish individuals, but by men honestly preoccupied with family and friends. We see the dangers that we rush into, but cannot afford to take the first step to a wider loyalty that yet (if all would take it) would serve our first friends well.

Similarly at the international level. We may all agree that we must love one another or (and?) die, but our loyalties are given first to those who are dear to us. If our enemies would not drop a nuclear bomb on us even if we dropped one on them, then we may safely do so; if they would incinerate our population in an act of futile vengeance, they are moral

62

imbeciles and so we had better attempt to get in first. And so we die. In these extremities it is just as well that our loyalties are not given so whole-heartedly to our nation-states.

A genuine altruism in us must come to terms with the vastly increased sphere of our endeavours, the vast increase in our destructiveness. It is not egoism that is our problem here: egoists would not 'defend' themselves with nuclear bombs. It is our genuine, heartbroken love for others that engenders war (amongst other causes): we are prepared to die, as well as to kill, for cause. Our ancestors, to leave us here at all, had to be concerned for their immediate family and friends, had to want not to murder, had to be moved to help at least in some extremities. When faced by creatures of another tribe, behaving in unfamiliar ways, we are not blocked so readily from following through our rage. We do not recognize their 'appeasement gestures', their reminder to us that they are fellow creatures, not just objects of our hatred. Of course, though gestures differ, there are common human traits: no one conveys surrender by bared teeth, hunched shoulders, and hands held out, shaped into talons. But the details change, and we misunderstand and take offence at the very things that were intended to avert offence. Patas and gelada monkeys don't get on, since patas flee aggression and gelada cringe. Hamadryas and anubis females can learn the other species' ways, but do not care for them (54). Presentation is, for primates, a common way of appeasing a dominant male, who mounts his male subordinates: but amongst bonnet macaques it is the dominant who is mounted (53). Such interspecies differences only exaggerate the differences of dialect and mannerism that obtain between subspecies, and even local groups. They are enough to ensure that until we have learnt each other's ways we will be less altruistic about aliens, and seize the upper hand more often than our own good would require.

Action, omission and extended care

These factors are worth remembering, but it is as well also to notice that modern wars are not obviously of a piece with intertribal quarrels. They are not powered by the fury of the individual combatants, uninhibited by their victims' efforts to appease. We fight wars because we are ready to forget ourselves and to obey our rulers, who are motivated by ideological urges. It is the wish to exercise power, and the human capacity actually to do so over large numbers, that is responsible for our bloody history. To blame wars on the activity of individual soldiers, as if a war was a collection of private quarrels, is to ignore the role of government and ideology.

Both we and other animals are more willing to hurt those unfamiliar to us than our dear familiars. We are also less willing to help them. For altruism has two facets: to help, and not to hurt. In that distinction we can find another aspect of 'true altruism'. If one were truly concerned about the welfare of others would one not be as concerned for their fate *not* at one's own hands as one is concerned not to hurt them? The wolf, who does not kill his rival when he might, still need not feel any impulse to aid his rival: I will not kill, but need not help to live. The end result of killing or of letting-die is just the same: the victim's death. Animals, even predators, do not treat all other animals indiscriminately as prey. Some spiders and the like have no compunction about killing and eating their own kind, but even they have developed rituals which permit mating and child-rearing to continue. More social kinds do not fight if they can help it, do not fight to the limit. But they need not help each other. Ruthless fighters are not evolutionary successes: they are likely to get hurt themselves, to hurt others of their own kindred, to waste time that could be spent on breeding and child-rearing. It does not 'pay' to fight on without limit – victors always teeter on the brink of sudden defeat by a victim driven to despair (96). But on the other hand it is hard to see how saintly altruism, dedication to another's good, could 'pay' and be preserved unless those who profit from the endeavours of the 'saint' are themselves close relatives. Members of the local group may care for each other (but there may be some pressure also to form factions in such groups, and so at length to split them), but any more extensive concern seems unlikely. Not all animals kill all strangers (though they will be readier to kill them than familiars), but few animals will comfort strangers in distress, or defend them from an enemy.

Two possible exceptions come to mind. Birds may give warning cries when predators are around that benefit all prey in hearing distance, even with some increased risk to the noisy bird. Dominant wolves may defend subordinates against their own closest rivals.

For birds the evolutionary point may be that birds who warn do not risk much, and may indeed increase their own chances by startling flocks of other birds into revealing motion – it's safer in a crowd (fish swim in shoals for a similar reason). It does not follow, I repeat, that this is the bird's motive: enough that predators are enemies, and all prey are allies in this matter (not in all). It is possible for patterns of behaviour to grow up that actually benefit more creatures than one's relatives. These are stable in evolutionary terms because they do benefit one's relatives, but that need not be why one follows them. Similarly our concern for what is familiar, or similar to what is familiar, may benefit creatures who are not related to us. Cuckoos profit from this fact. To say that this is an evolutionary 'mistake' is pointless, unless we wish to say also that our intellectual gifts, which far transcend what is necessary for our stock's survival, are also a 'mistake'. Mistakes are possible only where there is a conscious goal which we have failed to hit: if Nature has a goal we do not know what it is, and may as well conclude that She wishes us to have surplus affection and altruistic care as that She has made an error in the course of designing purely chauvinistic beasts.

Dominant wolves defend subordinates: maybe they do so only because it pays them individually to weaken their own closest threat, their 'second in command' (though see below). At least this may remind us that even those for whom we do not care may be an aid to us against a common enemy: we are adept at seeing the possibilities of the relationships between others. My enemy's enemy is my friend (for now). If we are to manage such a grasp of power politics we must be able to be aware of more distant relations, mediated to us through a common friend or enemy. So beasts may co-operate to overthrow a dominant male or to preserve an oligarchy each of whom is weaker singly than some upstart.

In all these ways we are made freer of our friendship than at first seems likely. Among human animals one further pattern emerges. We are astonishingly ready to share, to give. Wolves too will share a kill, and hunting dogs carry food home to their cubs and their guards. Chimpanzees, it seems, will beg and give a share of meat. Human beings, pre-eminently, forge and maintain society by giving things. The big men of early societies were big precisely in that they acquired goods to share them out again. To be impoverished is to have nothing left to give. It may be that our ancestors acquired this disposition when they turned to hunting: meat, being more concentrated and portable, is more readily shared than are plants. But our evidence for this is minimal: enough that we have a disposition not merely not to kill our companions, but to give to them. This may be an extension of the pattern seen in other primates, of comforting and grooming those who are in distress, but we have carried it, it seems, further than any other animal. Our lives are built on mutual support and

65

recompense. Reverse a cliché: we do not give because we love our friends; we love our friends, they are our friends, because we give to them (106).

The Kampucheans, after all, may not be quite so distant from our natural loves. They are, to be sure, of another stock, but they may call upon our generosity as well as on our rational grasp of their distress. If they, and all the other victims of the troubled world, do not get all the help they might, that may indeed be because we are still, for our sanity, forgetful of those troubles when they do not touch us close. But only ideologues can claim that evolutionary theory makes it clear that distant miseries do not count with us.

One final feature of our human condition: despite the cultural and racial differences of which I have spoken, we are still one species. Somehow we have avoided the inbreeding and racial selectivity that might have been expected to produce as many species of hominid as there are of baboon. Why have we stayed an interbreeding whole (or grown to be one, if we once were not)?

Chapter 7

SEXUALITY

Cultural and generic difference

The time is past when we could seriously believe that animals
are sexually rapacious and promiscuous. Judges may continue
to assert that rapists have behaved 'like animals', but it is
quite unclear what animal (apart from man) they are supposed
to resemble. Animals generally mate as the culmination of a
shared ritual, which in some (not all) species is itself a prelude
to the cares of parenthood. There are exceptions: mallards
without a lawful mate may force a female, and her established
mate responds by mating with her without ritual. In Calhoun's
'behavioural sink' (a population boom amongst confined rats)
all rituals lapse: nests are not built in order, young are
abandoned, males try to copulate with males, and females are
forced and bitten (12). But this is not how rats behave in
ordinary circumstances. Forced copulation is a rarity, and a
symptom of derangement. What is not clear is that it ever
equals *rape*. The roots of rape need not lie buried in behavioural sinks (although they may).

There is a popular, arch description of 'the loves of
animals' which is calculated to enrage most anthropologists
and ethologists. Elephants, some say, are romantic lovers,
using their trunks to fondle and to kiss. Lorenz sometimes
describes his ganders and jackdaws as engaging in affairs, as
though the gander were an adulterous commercial traveller
(63). The recent vogue for sociobiology has produced many
similar equations (though with opposite intent). Barash de-
clares, of humming birds who permit females access to certain
preferred flowers only on condition of copulation, that 'the
facts are analogous to human prostitution' (2) - which, so far
as it is true, is wholly uninteresting, or interesting only for the
social myopia its author displays (prostitution, strictly so
called, is not an evolutionary adaptation, but a patriarchalist
catastrophe). Again: certain South American birds like the
jacana are unusual in being 'polyandrous'. The ethologist who
reports this seems to equate this behavioural pattern with
Tibetan polyandry: both may be described as cases of 'many
brothers' sharing one wife' (52). It is but a step to the
tendentious claim that all cultural differences are founded on
or reflect genetic predisposition.

There are, accordingly, three attitudes to take toward

'the loves of animals'. The first, 'romanticism': Darwin postulated that such male and female birds as do not breed simply do not please each other - tastes differ, after all. The second, 'objectivism': looking only to the actual results (observable by anti-animists), some sociobiologists equate all human institutions with instinctual patterns. The third, 'humanism': anthropologists insist that jacana are no more polyandrous, coyotes no more monogamous, bull seals no more have harems, than are pandas vegetarian (their diet is not a cultural choice, embodying a way of living).

Romanticism should not be dogmatically denied. The particular explanation for non-breeding birds that Darwin offered can be refuted: C. B. Moffat pointed out (73) that if first one and then another of a breeding pair is eliminated the loss is at once made good from the pool of unmated birds, and two birds that, by Darwin's guess, had simply not pleased each other not so long before are very soon in orderly possession of a nesting site. The facts of the case make clear that what matters is possession of a territory, not (or not only) personal attachment. This piece of careful observation and experiment is worth any amount of objectivist rhetoric, but of course it does not require us to think that the birds do not think *anything* about their situation and their mates. It is only that they do not think of them in quite the way that Darwin guessed. Neither should humanism be rejected out of hand. An ideological dispute has muddied the waters here: all those who suggest that human groups may have significant genetic differences (significant in that they predispose to, or predetermine, cultural and behavioural differences) are classifiable as racialists. And it is true that human readiness not to remember the reality (as individual lives) of creatures who do not share our traits is such that anyone should be hesitant to fuel it further. But the discovery that there are genetic differences between groups, that there are subspecies of humanity, may serve instead to remind us that creatures who do not share all our traits may none the less be worthy of respect. Humanists surely do not intend to imply that if Tibetans *were* a different subspecies, even a different species, we should feel ourselves entitled to oppress them. Racialist ideology is not, I think, well combated by seeming to deny the facts and adopting, covertly, a speciesist ideology. Such practices bring humanism into disrepute: unfairly so.

It is not necessarily illiberal to wonder if genetic differences underlie the cultural. Different psychological types may be approved in different cultures, and in so far as those types correspond to different genotypes (which they may not do exactly, if at all), such different gene-structures may obtain an 'advantage' in evolutionary terms. Some cultures allow added opportunities to those afflicted with wanton ferocity, or those inclined to dissociation and trance, or those who can live according to a mechanical and supposedly dispassionate reason. Such characters may breed more successfully than their rivals, and so be 'selected' by the choices of a society increasingly inhabited by individuals predisposed to maintain those choices. This may be so, but there is little evidence that in fact such preferred character types *do* breed more successfully or that (if they do) our various cultures have yet been in stable existence long enough to have much evolutionary effect. It may be that there are significant genetic differences between populations that are the result merely of genetic drift, having no evolutionary advantage. It seems much more probable that we are still the common heirs of hunter-gatherers turned agriculturalists. Those who point to cultural differences usually seem unaware of their own history: there have been Caucasian polyandries as well as Tibetan, and though the Yamomamo are perhaps innately disposed to psychopathic ferocity it is barely two centuries since European males behaved with a brutality towards their wives and children that at least equals the Amerindian, and not half a century since we Europeans tried to destroy the racial minorities of our lands, fire-bombed Dresden, poisoned Japan and defoliated Vietnam. We are all, plainly, capable of almost anything.

I therefore share the humanist suspicion that a search for a genetic underlay for social difference is a waste of time (84). Cultural practices are not innate in men, or even in the higher mammals. I can see no reason to suppose that my children could not have been brought up to be good Amerindians, even good Aborigines. We are a versatile species, and any difficulties that may be imagined in socializing children to an alien environment will usually be obviously physical (they feel the cold or the heat more than their well-adapted cousins). This is not to say that nothing in their temperament can be innate, but only that such inborn differences do not seem to preclude successful membership of many different societies. It is clearly possible to find out what range of blood-groups (say) is found in any given society; it is not clearly possible to find out what character-types are found, because those types are not clearly defined, nor would it be possible (in practice) to insist that people were predetermined or predisposed to manifest such characters. To find this out is no discovery.

But how does all this happen? If non-human animals are genetically programmed, how does it happen that human animals are not? Where did this thing, culture, come from? How did it get started in a world where every life was laid down in the operations of the individual's genes? Believers in a special creation of humankind, or the miraculous insertion of souls in living matter, have an answer to this question, but most of us would need some convincing before we accepted such a radical discontinuity in the way things are.

Ritual and human choice

The mating of non-human animals is governed by 'ritual', in the technical sense of stereotyped behaviour patterns (borrowed from practical motor patterns) which are themselves innate: that is, in many cases, individual animals do not need to have seen the mating ritual to carry it out themselves. Ethologists have postulated that such rituals may evolve to mediate the opposite impulses to mate and to attack the other animal. Human mating customs, on the other hand, are enormously diverse and are internalized by example and precept. Even the mating position is fixed, in part, by mutual preferences ranged over the positions that are culturally approved.

Human rituals have cultural meanings: the sexual act is not, for human animals, merely a release of semen in a prepared receptacle (or if it is, that too has its own meaning). The partners are engaged in a demonstration of the value of certain modes of relationship. The medieval Rabbi who weekly enacts the union of God and the Shekhina, the tantric yogi who draws kundalini to the thousand-petalled lotus, the patriarch who lays himself upon his lawful wife, the lover who must shut her eyes against a light too bright to bear - all these are doing more than copulate. For human beings sex is always in the head, and shudders in the loins of little note. Romance is a human artefact, a medley of medievalism and the nuclear family and fear of flying. If it is asked what two lovers are doing, the reply may be that they're expressing independence of parental standards, acquiring peer-group status, seeking mystical experience, comforting the distressed, making babies, trying out position thirty-two. 'The sexual act' remains through all these transformations, but it is not the only thing the partners are doing, and in comparison with other things they do it is of little interest.

One further humanistic point: for beasts the sexual objects are determined. Of course things may go wrong: human-reared animals may be imprinted by the human form (like

Lorenz's goslings (63)), and only turn to their conspecifics with reluctance. But such disturbances are just that, anomalies. The patterns which excite the sexual appetite, or provoke mating behaviour, are innate or else learnt (imprinted) early. Insects may be enticed to mate with orchids, and presumably feel no disappointment, but they must sometimes get their partners right (or else there will not be many insects left). By contrast, it is said, what counts as a sexual object for human beings is profoundly personal. Anything may be taken by the individual as the object that will satisfy the sexual urge: there is no norm in human sexuality, as there is for beasts.

How might we respond to this? There need be no dispute about the facts: beasts must normally mate with members of the other sex, but they may also be attracted into sexual responses by orchids, human beings, members of the same sex or mere objects. Anything may be a sexual object, but presumably nothing will be that does not embody the pattern that releases this behavioural mode. This may be literally an *innate* releasing mechanism, or else one imprinted early on the animal, in obedience to the implicit ruling 'Fall in love with things like *this* . . .'. Beasts sometimes have to fall for 'the wrong objects', with which they have no hope of posterity. We could extend this account to cover human beings as well. Beauty, it has been said (65), is a releasing mechanism (though one's own idea of what it is will depend upon the culture and the family in which one is reared), and people do 'fall for' inappropriate things - inappropriate in that they are sterile. A species whose members did this too often would not long survive. But this 'animalistic' account of sexual response may seem to leave out the human valuation of the act, the personal decisions that issue in apparent 'perversion'. To be sexually excited by 'inappropriate' objects is to proclaim our liberation from the shackles of mere nature. 'Perversion' may not simply be a statistically rare derangement of an evolutionary norm, a response to the releasing mechanism that misses the evolutionary function of the behaviour, but a creative act, an exercise of human imagination quite other than the occasional misapplication of animal instinct.

On this account little is gained from comparing the incidence of sodomy in rats and baboons and men. Amongst baboons (and others) males may be mounted in a dominance display; amongst rats such 'homosexuality' may mark the decay of ritual. Amongst men the meaning of the act will vary from culture to culture, individual to individual: it says something, and something (maybe) personal. To take a more extreme example: necrophiliacs cannot usefully be assimilated to animals who, when frustrated of more appropriate objects, will attempt to mate with yet more schematized models of the proper partner.

The humanistic analysis emphasizes the personal choice of the agent as a significant element in what happens, an emphasis that most probably must lead to the transcendental Kantianism of an earlier chapter. A more biological approach, acknowledging the humanistic point for what it is worth, might be that human beings are in some ways more cohesive entities. That is to say that whereas beasts may be sexually 'deranged' without displaying any other derangements, a human being so badly off target as a necrophiliac must be very badly disturbed in other ways: all his behavioural modes are likely to misfire; it is not one aspect of his life that is off evolutionary target, but his whole life (40). Why this should matter to us (if at all) is another story.

The primary revolt 'against nature' to which humanistic thinkers have pointed is the ban on incest. Here, one might say, is the express denial that the paradigm 'sexual object', the pattern for all later sexual attraction, is to be treated as a sexual object at all. Whereas the fetishist proclaims human autonomy by making anything a sexual object (the masochist even finds delight in pain), so the moralist proclaims our opposition to nature by putting the most 'natural' sexual object out of bounds.

Fetishism, one may suspect, is a sadder and less autonomous mode of behaviour than existential humanists imply, but the main dispute is about incest. It certainly seems natural to suppose that beasts do not discriminate in their selection of sexual partners. Our domestic animals show no hesitation about son-mother or sibling-sibling or father–daughter matings. The ban on incest has therefore been hailed as the moment when humanity distinguished itself from mere nature, by deciding to give daughters and sisters away rather than keep them as wives (I am not unaware that this account is sexually biased). This decision does not rest on the supposedly bad effects of inbreeding: in fact, such bad effects are rather a consequence of the ban than its cause – for any harmful recessive genes would be eliminated from the gene pool in a very few generations of inbreeding (7). For the humanistic scholar the decision is a cultural one, a device for binding disparate groups together and turning against mere nature as a guide.

The ethologists' discovery that inbreeding is rather rare amongst non-human species in the wild, and that chimpanzees (not uniquely) appear to operate a ban on son-mother or sibling incest (father-daughter incest, obviously, cannot be banned when no father is known as such), may come as a surprise. The ban even *appears* to be innate: Lucy Temerlin, although presenting herself for ventral (NB) intercourse with any visiting male human rejected all embraces by her foster-father and his son (92). That, indeed, is the form that the ban takes: female chimpanzees repel their brothers (not always successfully). Such an intensive rejection of the too familar male may be, as it was in Lucy's case, associated with distress: rejection of one's own familiar friend may seem like hostility, but to appease the injured party may be to invite the same attention yet again. It is not unimaginable that such complexities of emotion lie at the root of our guilts. But the examples that ethologically inclined anthropologists adduce to suggest that human beings too have their instinctive barriers against inbreeding do not altogether meet the case. It may be that kibbutz children do not usually marry those with whom they grew up, but the aversion (if there is one) is that of boredom with the over-familiar, not Lucy's terror. Nor is it universally true that children brought up together do not mate or marry. Much more is owed to cultural expectation than ethologists sometimes suggest (77).

Again: ethologists have used the term 'incest' a little carelessly. What is notable about human mating-practices is not that siblings do not mate, but that there are whole structures that dictate who marries whom, structures reflected in other rituals and in story. It seems quite pointless to explain such ramifications of cross-cousin matrimony and taboo by referring to female unwillingness to accept their brothers' advances. It may be that our ancestors lived in such groups as macaques now favour, combining the connectives of descent and alliance (37). But what they built upon those beginnings seems to have little enough to do with evolutionary thought.

None the less it is worth considering the opposing evolutionary forces that constrain us all. On the one hand, we must find creatures of our own kind sexually attractive (how else is a species to survive?); on the other, we must prefer creatures of a slightly unfamiliar sort, for outbreeding offers the genetic 'advantage' of increased variety. This latter impulse, to lust after the (relatively) alien, is the genetic or social imperative that has kept our various and dispersed species as one species: we can still breed together because our ancestors have always fancied something new, and because at some point some cultural genius created the elements of the kinship structures that govern descent and alliance.

Sexuality

The mammalian problem

In this context, of cultural invention that draws on innate or readily acquired predisposition, compare the various marital arrangements men have made with the mating practices of our cousins. Simply to equate these, overtly, or by covert application of the same terms to both (polyandry, harem, wife), is unwise, as it allows the cultural prejudices of the scholar to predetermine a view of beasts. But men are mammals, and must share some things, even if only problems.

The mating arrangements of mammals vary, but practically all mammals share one feature: the females are the primary parents, and the mother-child bond is the primary bond. Solitary mammals, such as hamsters or lemurs or (at least in our society) cats, mate without permanent attachment and leave all parenting to the mother. Some coati and wild boars continue solitary, if male, but the females group together with their offspring. Amongst wildebeest and coati the males may form into cohorts, maintaining themselves independently of the mother-children groups. Amongst zebra and hamadryas, some of the males move from their cohorts into the female band: a form regularly called 'polygyny' (the hamadryas case presents additional features I will deal with later). Dikdiks and gibbons have a 'monogamous' system, one male paired with one female in something more like the normal bird-system. Amongst wolves and mongooses only the dominant pair breed, their companions revolving around that central royalty, their sexuality suppressed by fear (in which case they may copulate out of sight) or by 'psychological castration' (7). Finally, there may be groups of male and female together, surplus males being formed into cohorts on the outer rim: as rhesus monkeys, or chimpanzees. These examples, it should be said, are mostly debatable: different scholars may read the relationships a little differently, and even creatures of a single species may have different customs in different areas. But we need not investigate (though others may) the details of the differences, so as to match them with the differing environments in which they dwell. My point here is simply that the central problem of mammals is - what to do with the males?

Consider lions (5): our popular picture of a lion pride is of a maned despot and his admiring wives and young. But if instead we follow the fate of a male cub a different view emerges. Female cubs may stay with the pride to which they were born, though some will be driven out to face life by themselves. All male cubs are driven out, and either live

74

solitary or stay loyal to their brothers till they are old enough to drive an old male from his haven in a pride and take his place, for a year or two, till they in their turn are driven out. Or take red deer: the females have permanent herds, mothers being dominant over their offspring; the males herd separately, except that at rutting time they get themselves 'harems'. Is this situation, and a host of others, quite what male ethologists have usually supposed? Does it lend weight to patriarchalism, the view that females just need masters?

Again: human females are unusual in being 'permanently receptive to sexual advance', not merely at a monthly oestrus or at rutting time. One explanation has been that this is how they trap the males into staying with them to care for their young. It is unclear why it is assumed so quickly that males, if given half a chance, would hurry off. Nor is it clear why permanently sexy females would do much to keep males faithful to the mothers of their children. In fertile species, where little time is spent on child-rearing, it may 'pay' males to scatter their seed in many females. Where it is difficult to rear children to maturity the mothers need help, either from other mothers or from fathers too. Let us reverse the story: suppose that males very much want to be part of the continuing family group, but are thrown out into the world. How shall they get back again? If human males were as impressive as gorillas they might manage to be awe-inspiring despots without the backing of the male cohort. Or they might attempt the hamadryas' trick of kidnapping infant females and rearing them as wives (56). But one technique for being loved is simply being lovable, and this trick is turned by the prolongation of sexual interest in the woman. In other words, women are potentially receptive all the time because it gives them (the individual women) a reason to want males around and a chance to choose when to be receptive. This in turn serves the evolutionary function of providing greater care and protection for the children - against the other males, quite possibly. Those of our ancestors who wanted males around most of the time bred more successfully than those who threw them out before the cubs were born. The dominance routines of the male cohort will concern me later. There need be no denial that this form of life has persisted in the human species, that many males (perforce, or by their choice) have made a life among males. But there has always been this other option of finding one's way back into a family, by being attractive, by being seen to be a possibly good spouse and father. Not all men like exclusively male company, *pace* the patriarchalists (7). The matrilineal descent lines and the alliances of the evicted males are the two foundations of mammalian life, but we need not draw patriarchalist conclusions from the facts of our evolution. Feminist ethology (which is not to say *matriarchalist* ethology) is an option too.

Is chastity a natural virtue or an artificial one? The normal use of sexuality is to unite and (in many species) bond the parents of another generation, not necessarily in monogamous pairs. To that extent we may expect that the normal operation of the drives involved will be hedged about with ritual and sometimes inhibition. But male dominance routines may alter cases. Hamadryas females do not scruple to retire behind a rock and mate with males other than their self-proclaimed despot: on returning from the assignation they groom the male whose 'harem' they inhabit. Their fidelity is not a natural thing, but a concession made (in public) to keep their pet quiet. We should not be misled by male strength even in those species where the males are stronger individuals than the females: that strength is directed chiefly against other males, and the females continue with their lives regardless. Even if it were true that 'The average male can always thrash the average female' that does not make males bosses. Why should we consider such males to be the happy owners of a harem, any more than are lions?

Chastity as a disposition not to be perverse, not to waste sexual energy elsewhere than in such practices as maintain the community, is natural enough. As the demand for total fidelity in females it can be natural only if that fidelity is a response to the experienced value of the males involved. As obedience to the requirements of the incest-structure, a cultural artefact that is not exhausted by simple aversion to siblings' copulation (if that exists), it is an invention older still than prudence. And what beasts think of it we can still only guess.

The sex war

I have suggested that it is unclear that males should have any particularly strong wish to desert their family group. In fact there is a possible argument for this. Females invest relatively large amounts in their offspring, males relatively little. Having invested so much, the females must see that their investment pays: it does not 'pay' a female to desert her young in order to acquire more (except in exceptional circumstances). It may 'pay' males not to stick around a particular female and offspring, but to try to beget more offspring. The point is not that 'Women are monogamous, men are poly gamous', but that males may have more offspring if they do not occupy themselves with child-rearing.

It may therefore be concluded that females should 'invest' in male offspring, thereby acquiring more grandchildren. If they were to do so, however, there would be too few females in the second generation to give more than a few males any chance of offspring. The 'stable strategy' turns out to be to produce more or less equal numbers of male and female offspring (though the details of this continue to exercise researchers).

The turns of the argument are a reminder not to take first thoughts as final. 'A male may have more offspring if he does not remain with the first' (though the male's capacity for sexual activity has been much exaggerated - ejaculation is a costly business!): but what matters in the end is how many surviving offspring he has. Certainly in prolific species a male can reckon (as it were) that enough will survive without his help; but where only one or two offspring are born at a single birth, and they need care and assistance over many years, the male who does not desert may have more surviving offspring than the one who does. The usual problem of the 'freeloader' may emerge: the male who insinuates his offspring into stable groups may 'win' for a while, but if he has too many surviving offspring with the same trait freeloading becomes impossible. It is likely that other males will have evolutionary cause to detect and exclude such irresponsible males.

Does this show that patriarchalist jealousy is after all the evolutionary norm? Not necessarily so. Whether it 'pays' a male to prevent any other male from begetting offspring on the mother of his offspring will depend on how many females are available, how closely related the other male is, and (most important) how much help can be expected from that other male in the protection of the family group. We can in fact expect that males will not much object to familiar males' mating with 'their' females, so long as those males do assist the group. It may be, of course, that dominant males will insist on 'exclusive possession' at the peak of oestrus.

So males need not be deserters, and need not be possessive. Females, similarly, need not be monogamous: for though it will not pay them to desert their offspring, it may be possible to rely on males and female relatives to 'aunt' the first child while they have another (see below). And it may 'pay' them to enlist the support of males other than the actual father by mating with them.

In this way it may eventually turn out that individual

males and females invest very much the same amount in their offspring and have very similar reasons not to reserve their sexual activity to a single partner. In short, the family group or 'group marriage' may well be the optimum, co-operative solution (19). Whether it emerges in any given species will depend upon that species's situation, and upon mere historical accident. Patriarchy of our familiar sort is certainly a possibility, but it is not the only one to have roots in our primate and mammalian heritage.

The real moral to be drawn is that where so many possibilities beckon it is the ability to look ahead and to adapt our ways that has the greatest evolutionary gain.

Chapter 8

PARENTHOOD

'Tis time for deeper passions; now I am a mother, more impressive crimes are expected.   Seneca, *Medea*

Parents and aunts

Parents must care for their children. That is natural law, according to the ancients. Where young things are born weak with much to learn they will survive to reproduce more often if some guardian cares for them. And how could anyone have an evolutionary interest in doing so but those whose genes they bear – their parents? It has therefore never been very surprising that parents fight for their children's lives – though in a prolific species an 'advantage' might sometimes go to the mother who abandoned one litter to start a more favourable one. When the males have not been integrated into the matrilineal families they get no 'advantage' from paternal devotion; when they have, they too must play their part in the protection even if not in the nurture of the child.

But other animals than parents care for children. The case of the social insects, as I have already observed, offers no helpful parallel to mammalian practice, since the insects' reproductive system predisposes them to the evolution of sterile sisters and an exploited brood-queen ('exploited' only in functional terms: how the insects see the matter we don't know). Even creatures of another species may be able to take advantage of the parental responses that would normally be directed toward the real offspring: cuckoos rely upon a parent bird's impulse to fill up gaping mouths, and perhaps upon the parent's preference for larger eggs and young. Some apparent 'evolutionary mistakes' turn out not to be: certain South American birds, tormented by botflies, either nest near wasps or are parasitized by cowbirds (on the cuckoo model): either gives protection against botflies (2). Interspecies co-operation can evolve.

Within a species it evolves more readily. Ostriches, interestingly, lay eggs in other ostriches' nests, so that any given couple are caring for eggs that are at least not the female's. As the male birds also mate with solitary females whose only chance of evolutionary success is to lay an egg in some established couple's nest, the extra eggs may sometimes be the

male's. Even established nest-mothers lay some eggs elsewhere. They do not keep their eggs all in one basket, and by
accepting others' eggs in their own basket they offer their own
eggs a small protection against predators.

But the most interesting cases are supplied by the higher
mammals. Birds, both male and female partners, generally
care for their own young. Love-birds even work at being good
spouses, slowly perfecting their techniques for avoiding squab-
bles (26). Such models for monogamy are the exception among
mammals, whose females are much more adapted to the
nurture of the young. Where the young take a deal of nurturing
it is plainly difficult for any single creature to provide that
care, and the commonest unit of parental care is the female
lineage, with or without intruded males. Other members of
such a troupe will wish to care for the young. Such 'aunting'
has been observed in rhesus monkeys and in elephants: a
primate, but not just a primate, pattern. J. H. Crook, noting
the rivalry to get hold of some youngster, remarks that 'aunts
are persistent animals' (23). Such efforts to find a child to care
for make it clear that parenting is not a thing forced on such
creatures: it is what they want to do. Aunts who have had
some practice on another's child may rear their own offspring
more successfully; mothers who allow their children to be
cuddled, groomed or fed by others are freed to follow other
impulses. Practice, and the presence of a peer-group, even
allows Harlow's maimed monkeys to advance a little from
their first, psychotic attitude to their own young (45). Such
caring groups, not nuclear families, are the evolutionary
background out of which we grew. Porpoise females assist
each other in giving birth, and help the young up to the
surface. They similarly help unconscious adults (porpoise and
human) (48).

Males, if they have a part to play in this, may also act as
aunts. Hamadryas baboons, particularly, strive to adopt young
females to rear up a 'harem' (or a family), and may snatch up
youngsters to use them as shields in confrontations with more
dominant males. Woolly monkeys tolerate, and, by the signs,
enjoy the play-fighting and cuddling of the young. Barbary
apes reward and punish youngsters, and male apes have been
observed teaching them to walk (76). Male function, however,
is more generally protective than nurturing: the fringe of
young adult males that surround a baboon troupe (which in
other species might form an independently foraging male
cohort) function as watchmen, guardians and placatory sacrifice, until they (or a few of them) manage to re-enter the
central, largely female group. The sons of dominant females

have more chance of this re-entry. Even (or perhaps especially) dominant males who have been accepted into the female
group, act as protectors: as a patas monkey chasing a jackal.
Such a sexual 'division of labour' (a misnomer for what is not a
cultural artefact) between the nurturing female and the protective male is not exact (females are protective too, and
males may cuddle), and it certainly does not offer any reason
to suppose that human society should be modelled on the
values of middle-class America (*pace* E. O. Wilson) (104).

We are equipped, in short, to care for and protect the
young of other parents. This does not conflict with evolutionary theory: in the small groups where we were bred most
young will be related to the agent, and the releasing mechanism for parental or quasi-parental care (the 'cuteness gestalt')
will normally elicit behaviour that preserves the genes for just
such a disposition. That is not, I emphasize, the creature's
motive for her acts, only the evolutionary function of the acts
aimed, in the creature's consciousness, at having one to care
for (which is not necessarily to say, at that youngster's good:
aunts may disregard the youngster's interests).

Antagonism and aggression

Unfortunately, it may also happen that incoming males, born
in another troupe, may gain an 'advantage' by killing off the
young who have been fathered by another, unrelated male.
Hanuman langurs and lions, and even gorillas, have been
observed to kill cubs in this way. Lionesses, indeed, miscarry
their own cubs, apparently to make room quickly for the new
lion's seed. Langur females help each other against the incoming males (2). Clearly cuteness need not rule out killing. Such
acts may be less likely where the fathers are from the same
troupe, or from a closely related one. But if such an impulse to
dispose of aggravating little creatures exists at all, its sudden
eruption even against one's own offspring cannot be ruled out.
If this happened too often, such behaviour would eliminate
itself from the evolutionary line, whether or not some other
creatures managed to maintain the species. It could be argued
that taking children from their parents lest they be battered
to death is precisely to perpetuate the problem, by allowing
offspring of the would-be batterers to survive and to become
(perhaps) such batterers in their turn.

Such covert appeals to let things be, let 'nature' find a
way, are not, it seems, quite justified. Why should we assume
that 'baby-batterers' form a class apart, uniquely predisposed
to violence? Environmental factors are more obvious, and

more easily altered: if inexperienced parents are to care for infants in deprived environments, expected to sleep intermittently and be on call all day, the only surprise is that more babies are not beaten. Things are made worse, no doubt, by a punishing and child-hating ideology, and some few baby-beaters may be psychopaths, but the most earnestly liberal parent in the most comfortable environment, with partners and friends to call upon, may sometimes feel pure rage and be within an inch of violence.

But how is it that we aren't well-equipped to care for infants all the time, if that is what we do? Perhaps it is that we are now required to care for them much longer than we are equipped to bear. Or perhaps it would have been the whole community that cared for them, even though there was a special tie between the mother and her child (a tie that lasts into adult life at least among chimpanzees). Primates generally are equipped to live in a relatively stable group composed of long-lived individuals of all ages and both sexes (53). What happens within that frame must vary. Do the males display possessive jealousy, associated maybe with a fear that they may be displaced? Do young males flee the group, or stay in fear, or suppress their sexuality, or grow up to join such new groups as may form from the old one as it grows too large? Humane patterns are not impossible, though they may depend upon the character of the leading members of the group.

Jealousy is perhaps the crucial fault. It is not universal. Though some males maintain a hold upon a band of females, and fight off other males who seek a share, this is not always true. And where it is we may interpret the behaviour as protective, not aggressive. In some groups only the dominant male mates, though he may not enforce his claim with anything more than a symbolic nip. In others, the dominant male mates with the females at the peak of their oestrus, when they are most likely to conceive, but does not prevent any other matings. In other groups again there seems no sign that the dominant male is especially interested in sex. These differences seem to occur even within species (which should not surprise us much), though chimpanzees appear to be promiscuous and baboons rigorously hierarchical. We need not think that we are doomed to jealous and possessive ways.

Not doomed to them, perhaps: but jealousy does still occur, and we can perhaps find its root in 'the aggressive impulse'. Ethological suggestions that 'aggression' has an instinctual root have had a bad press. Ethologists have been interpreted as saying (some of them may think that they are saying) that war, murder, rape are unavoidable, that we want to hurt each other, that only a police-state can control the war of all against all, that we had better arrange for gladiatorial bouts to relieve aggressive fury. This does not seem to be to the point. 'Aggression', in ethological jargon, covers any display or threat or carefully inhibited contest. Injuries occur, and even deaths, but the impulse to 'aggression' is no more than the impulse to make a good show before one's fellows, to try one's weight. Such contests do not, most often, employ the animal's most dangerous weapons nor in the most dangerous way. Such competition rests upon the unformulated principle that the winner of the contest gets some other good: but the good thing itself is not fought over, not 'scrambled' for (103). What there is reason to suppose is that animals do not fight only to obtain such other goods as food or mates or shelter, but also for the sake of the display. To be deprived of any rival for a while builds up frustration in a captive cichlid (a fish) even if he has all other comforts. Hamsters run mazes for the reward of a good fight.

We do not always fight because we are frustrated in other areas - though we may then fight harder; we are frustrated, sometimes, because we have no 'fight' on hand. Tom-cats fight to establish a rank-order which does not match the preferences of females: dominance does not give any sexual monopoly (65). Birds fight in musical displays, and humans in verbal, elaborating their conceits beyond what is needed for a victory: academics know this well, even if contemporary fashion insists that the fights should be 'gentlemanly'. Humanistic responses to Lorenz's work on aggression are quite enough to demonstrate that human beings are aggressive! But the point of these displays is not to hurt or maim one's rival, but rather to establish one's own life within a social context. Robins need rivals just as they need mates. The fundamental principle of evolutionary ethology is that a pattern which is vital to the evolutionary success of a kind will be engaged in by the animal *for its own sake*, not merely as a hated means to some foreseen goal. Things can go wrong: our history is proof enough of that. Displays, attempts to carve a living place in our group, response to dominance or to appeasement, all may sometimes fail to keep their limits.

Patriarchalism

Accounts of aggression usually suggest that it is males that play these games, and this may be true, though females too have their own separate rank-orderings. But the mammalian male cohort maybe reflects the female lineage: each male,

83

after all, has had the experience of growing up beneath the sway of mother, and maybe a matriarch, who has then evicted him. Human psychology at least suggests that he may strive both to find a new 'mother' among the other males, and himself to dominate the lesser males - to recreate a parent-child relationship, in rivalry of the female lineage. Pederasty is the form of politics. This is, I emphasize, *human* psychology: some human societies arrange for new male initiates to be, for example, subincised (an operation that leaves the urethra exposed, and maybe with a hole in it). It is difficult not to see this as an attempt to create a symbolic womb that bleeds, and also to block off all memory of those early years when he was with the mothers. Human beings have, most probably, resources of symbolism that are denied even our closest cousins, but their psychology in this may not be all that different. Why should it be? The motives I have mentioned are not entirely rational, though they do require some grasp of the agent's own self and relationship with others. When a wolf 'inhibits' a victor's aggression by rolling over and presenting his neck for biting, his belly for washing, he says, in effect, 'I am a child.' When a hamadryas baboon adopts a young female the eventual result may be the creation of a 'harem', but we have no strong reason to think that the baboon intends more than the adoption of a child, the becoming a 'mother'. The male alliance, on which patriarchalists found all politics (94), is an ersatz copy of the sisterhood.

When males are incorporated in the family group as adults, we usually assume that it is to assure themselves of sexual satisfaction. This may indeed play a part, though other species manage sexual access for the males without such systems. Perhaps what is really at issue is the males' desire to become 'mothers'. If this is so it may explain why jealousy arises: after all, it need not diminish one male's sexual satisfactions that another male occasionally, or frequently, is entertained by the same female. His status as 'mother' is affected if it comes to seem to him that his females do not need him; his status as 'child' is affected if his females pay attention to others. One way in which human beings accommodate these tensions is by the institution of marriage, which does not seem to be paralleled in other animal species.

For the point about marriage is not that one male maintains a claim on one or more females, defending them against seduction by his rivals. The point is that the whole community, or especially the male cohort, enforces each male's 'rights'. I defend 'my' female(s) against seduction; I also defend yours. Patriarchalist society is the enforcement by the

84

male cohort of special claims upon the women. In this way each male is assured some chance of growing up to be a 'mother'. The backing of the cohort is crucial: male gorillas are awe-inspiringly larger than their females; human beings are not so dimorphic, and no single male has any clear chance of controlling even one, let alone more than one, of the available females (78) (though there may be charismatic males).

Within this distinctively (not universally) human institution the possibility of baby-battering increases. For marriage is not instituted for the welfare of the infants, but as a way of coping with the adult males and their wish to be simultaneously mothered (as they once were) and exclusive mothers. Children are rivals for the wives' affections. In a fully-fledged patriarchalism, where patrilineal descent has replaced the older matrilineal, hostilities increase. When there is only one wife, Laius and Oedipus are at war.

In following this I am suggesting that the complex of attitudes and desires that result so often in baby-battering and in child-hating practices can be seen as distortions created by patriarchalist institutions that have been adopted to cope with the emotional tensions of the one-time evicted males. It is unlikely that patriarchal marriage has yet existed long enough to create a species, or subspecies, genetically equipped to fit it; it is also unlikely that sociobiological theory could provide a convincing reason for the maintenance of the patriarchate. It is certainly not enough to say that males are genetically determined to care for their own children and to attempt to guard their 'own' females' chastity while making inroads on all other males' wives. There seems no reason why the ostrich phenomenon should not occur instead, or the group fellowship from which our kind has grown. Baboon troupes are united chiefly by the presence of infants. Anthropologists have pointed out that in some societies it is his sister's child that the male must care for, not any child that might be judged his own (84). To this sociobiologists have answered, ingeniously, that in a promiscuous society the sister's child is more likely to carry the male's genes than any other woman's is, and once such a relationship is established it is in the male's 'genetic interest' to encourage his sister's promiscuity (97). The response is an ingenious one, but it entirely fails to show that there is any genetic determination of the existence of such a society. Why do such males accept less by way of 'genetic advantage' than could be gained by full monogamy? Or if it is not clear that more could be gained monogamously, what becomes of the sociobiological explanation of that institution? It is worth remembering that we are a versatile kind, and that many different institutions may fulfil the genetically determined needs and wants we have – more or less.

Patterns of parental and marital behaviour are not innate, in men or monkeys. But they may rest upon patterns that are, at least, very readily acquired. The curious pathologies that render us so much less affectionate towards our young, so irrationally possessive about the attention that we are getting, may arise in part from cultural solutions to the problem of the male, but they could not develop in the ways they have unless they met some possibility of our genetic heritage. It is natural law that parents care for children: but there must also be some device that breaks the tight parental bond (98) – first because new offspring may require attention, and secondly because the line will not extend beyond a generation if the offspring do not grow up and form relationships of their own outside the parental bond. Sociobiologists have argued that it is to the parent's 'advantage' to get rid of a child a little before the child's own 'advantage' would require. Parental hostility thereby develops, a wish that the child would simply go away. Where society prevents this happening, where there is nowhere for the child to go, the tensions mount. Where the impulse to let the child go free is itself muted by the sort of jealousies I have described, and the child wants to go well before the parent can bear the loss, adolescent rebellion appears – a syndrome not obviously explicable by sociobiologists (though their ingenuity is almost unlimited).

One problem faced by parents, though, may have a biological ground: the screaming child. Undoubtedly, in our past a baby's crying earned some reward, most probably quite quickly (though nilgiri langurs leave them screaming). Babies that cry for food and comfort survive a little better than those that lie passively. But it must also sometimes have been vital that the child should lie quiet, lest predators or enemies take all the family. Dawkins absurdly describes the situation as one of blackmail ('Feed me or the bogey-bear will get you') (24), but the point is a genuine one. The desire to silence a crying child can become a desperate one, and many baby-batterers are, in their desperation, striving to do just that. Things are not helped by the fact that a child's impulse on being hurt is to appeal for help, to cling, precisely, to her parents, who are just enraged the more. Parents who could kill their children have, in our past, sometimes had more children in the end than those who could not.

If these difficulties, of genetic heritage and cultural adaptation, are as real as they seem, we cannot reasonably hope that the 'natural man' is as unfailingly and open-endedly patient, generous and self-giving as society and child-psychology textbooks require mothers in particular to be. The unspoken belief that mothers are somehow naturally equipped to dedicate themselves whole-heartedly to the care and nurture of small, demanding animals has been a prolific source of ill: if mother-love comes automatically, and is infinite, then mothers can do it all themselves, and if they can't, it must be that they are unwomanly.

If we can remember that we are animals, though versatile and culturally creative, we may step a little closer to humane society. We are evolved to live in relatively open groups, with members of many ages and both sexes. We need to be able to find our place in that group, testing ourselves against and with our rivals. If a parent, usually in this society a female, has no adult opposite to proclaim her own identity against, she is likely enough to 'take it out' on the child. If she must also cope with the infantile longings of her mate to be both mother and child she has that much less energy and help to deal with the child. If she is short of sleep, she is most probably deranged in any case. These features of our situation make it clear, I think, that ethological analysis of the human animal does not lead to a defence of modern Western marriage. If anything can be concluded from all this it must be that the (relatively) open group is where we are meant to be (80, 23).

Chapter 9

TERRITORY AND DOMINANCE

Territory

Two schools of thought contend in the matter of territory, aggression, dominance. On the one hand, those who think that men are peaceful and ungrasping creatures (were it not that civilization corrupts us all); on the other, those who rear up strong defences of modern capitalism on the basis of ethological observation. Both sides exaggerate, and pay little attention to reporting their opponents' views correctly. At times they end up saying the same things, and arguing that their own views are proved thereby. Thus, the dominance order of many animal groups is instanced both to show that animals are aggressive, and that they are not. The term 'aggressive' is now hopelessly obscure (96). Nor is it helpful to dispute whether animals are territorial or not without fixing on some relatively clear account of what it is to be territorial: chimpanzee groups may retreat, keeping themselves to themselves, or even attack other groups - does that make them territorial (32)? Not if the term means only an insistence on defending an area against incursion, but it is not wholly unnatural to extend it to cover any spatial distancing between individuals and groups - the chimpanzees carry their territory around with them (within limits).

My bias, as is probably plain, is to consider that human beings are indeed a kind of animal, and that 'culture is man's peculiarly elaborate way of expressing the vertebrate biogram' (22) (a biogram is the inborn programme for a kind's behaviour). But I am also biased toward a socialistic view of the possibilities of human community. What can be said of dominance-routines, and territorial behaviour? Are they the old Adam, or a figment of right-wing ideologues, or are they not so bad?

To begin at the beginning: solitary animals are not unsocial. Indeed it is almost the reverse that is true: animals that are generally seen in shoals or swarms are actually unsocial. The midges that gather in clouds are not (ethologists suspect) responding to each other's presence, but to other features of the environment, in a stereotyped way. They are all, individually, trying to stay within a particular favourable area. Fish may gather in shoals, responding to each other's presence, but not through any desire for social intercourse. Any strange

88

conspecific may join the shoal (in functional terms, to get cover against predators), whereas rats, for instance, would kill a stranger. Such fish are (weakly) social, but do not form a society: for that it is necessary to respond with a difference to members of the group; this may result in being solitary, in the sense that the animal in general lives away from other conspecifics. Such solitude cannot be absolute in any sexual species: somehow the normal barriers must come down. But if it exists at all, the chances are high that the creatures are taking account of each other's presence, and dispersing themselves accordingly.

Some popular accounts have made it seem that territorial animals maintain a constant barrier against all incursions, save of a potential mate. In fact the territorial phase need not be permanent, nor is it universal even among a territorial kind. Some birds do not win territories (and so do not breed), and they will be concerned to try to win them only in the breeding season. At other times they flock together. Vervets are territorial in some areas, not in others (54). Ethologists have speculated, with some plausibility, that territorial and flocking behaviour emerge in accordance with what is offered in the way of forage. A pair of birds may need fairly exclusive control of an area if they are to find enough food for their offspring; individual birds do not have the same need. Seasons too may change. Sometimes the breed will survive more effectively if all compete directly for the available forage, in a scramble competition (so some starve, the ones least able to win through); sometimes a contest which assigns available resources in some replica of a rationing system will provide the best evolutionary results. Both patterns are ingrained in the breed.

Territorial behaviour can also be ascribed to groups, though it is not always clear whether such groups actively defend their area or whether they merely restrict their wanderings to it (and other groups likewise restrict themselves). The result may be the same: an area is made available to members of that group, and to no other (103). But conditions change: elephants usually gather in matriarchal groups, but after famine, when many families have lost their leaders, vast herds may form instead (89).

Hierarchies

'Animals are all like werewolves' (66); they have different parts to play at different times, and in response (sometimes) to different cues. But these different behaviour patterns can sometimes be seen as modulations of a single theme. It seems reasonable to treat territorial and dominance behaviour in this way, as establishing relative and absolute hierarchies.

Those animal-kinds who have solved the problem of providing enough food for individuals to survive often enough to propagate the kind by parcelling the foraging area out, no longer share their unsocial cousins' attitudes. Other animals may breed together, but they do not otherwise treat conspecifics as very different from other objects in their environment. Territorial animals have the experience of being owners and of recognizing owners' claims (they need not be doing this in any very explicit or self-conscious way). They have in particular the experience of a relatively ritualized competition: owners make displays and rushes at intruders, and the intruders generally accept defeat. No evolutionary error here: intruders who tried to drive the owner out would run the risk of serious injury – better to retreat and try again elsewhere (or later on). I must emphasize that this need not be (almost certainly is not) the intruders' calculation: they accept the situation, and will defend their own territory in their turn. (It is not only males, by the way, that sometimes defend territories.)

What will such creatures do when it is time, seasonally or from sudden drought, to leave their territorial ambitions and form flocks? It might be possible for them simply to abandon contest competition, and instead to scramble for the scarce resources. But they may instead adopt an absolute hierarchy: some animals are dominant over others, not merely (or at all) by virtue of superior strength but by the appropriate cues and signals. Their dominance is not what human despots enjoy. They do not give orders to their subordinates, but only exclude them from favoured places, prevent their performing certain acts. Most members of the group will continue about their business without being troubled by the dominant: only those who seek to pre-empt the place or infringe the dignity of the dominant will be disciplined. Such dominant individuals have first call on resources; those at the very bottom of the heap may lose, as it seems, all will to live – at least, during famines. (It is well to remember that we are descended from such creatures as were ready to let their subordinates starve, while themselves remaining relatively well-fed.) They do not need to fight for food. A dominant rhesus, in E. O. Wilson's description, bears an odd resemblance to Aristotle's hero, the great-hearted man: 'head and tail up, testicles lowered, body movements slow and deliberate and accompanied by unhesitating but measured scrutiny of other monkeys that cross his path' (103). Dominants have dignity.

Why should their inferiors let themselves be bred out of the species? An earlier biological account assigned this habit to self-sacrifice for the species's good. Species whose less viable members were ready to go under rather than pull all down with them survived more effectively than species whose members all struggled to keep alive on resources that could only preserve a few. Similarly, hunter-gatherer groups whose elderly and sick accepted their abandonment would have the edge on groups that sought to cherish every useless mouth. Unfortunately, though such habits would indeed preserve a group during times of famine, it is very difficult to see how they could evolve. Any such aged altruists would be saving non-altruists as well - within a few generations all survivors would be non-altruists, undisposed to accept relegation. Since species do survive through years of famine by just such inegalitarian distribution of resources, some other mechanism must be involved. Amongst human beings cultural conditioning, and the extraordinary ability (or destiny) of human beings to see themselves as others do, will probably account for it. In other kinds it may simply be a by-product of what is generally an 'advantageous' strategy: subordinates do not 'profit' from forcing a confrontation, at least till they convince their rival that they are superior. In a famine they never get a chance to make their come-back.

What I have described is a genuine hierarchy. Not all dominance behaviour is so structured. Barnyard fowls, for whom the term 'peck-order' was first formed, do not always make a linear hierarchy: alpha dominates beta, who dominates gamma, who dominates alpha in turn. Only where the relationship is transitive is hierarchy established. And of course even if alpha is technically dominant over gamma, it may be that their relationship is more affectionate as well as more distant: it is *beta* that alpha must fear, and so alpha may make an ally of gamma. It is not unknown for relatively elderly primates to maintain a coalition against upstart youngsters who could defeat them, each of them one at a time. Even if defeated, the alpha male may retain his position, presumably because of the other creatures' habit of giving way, or (equivalently?) their respect for age (53).

In ordinary times the dominant animals may get a personal profit, as well as satisfaction, from treating their subordinates protectively or nurturingly. The evolutionary 'advantage' is also theirs, that by so doing they increase the percentage of creatures so disposed to kindliness in the next generation. Such groups are not structured only 'agonistically', by display and confrontation, but also 'hedonically', by grooming and playing

(14). Dominants enjoy being groomed subordinates like grooming. The presence of infants, who are not yet quite competitors and who are allowed great licence by their elders, also mutes such contests as may start. Macaques as well as hamadryas are reported to use infants as social buffers in their confrontations with possibly irascible superiors.

In peaceable times the dominants may protect infants and the weaker of their troupe. They may not always intend to: bull sea-lions patrol their 'harem', thereby preventing rash swimming when there are sharks about (31); but sea-lions are not so careful of their cubs' lives on other occasions as to make one think it matters all that much to them. Leonard Williams's woolly monkey, Jojo, on the other hand, systematically tested the branches of a spinney made accessible to the colony before he would permit the other monkeys to risk themselves there (101). This behaviour, together with the monkeys' capacity to recognize each other individually and to respond to each others' requests (for grooming, or a shared treat), suggests that he did intend to try the branches out in case one of his family fell.

Different dominants have different styles, and the whole feeling of a group may change when a new leader comes. Some may be hostile and overbearing (53). But in general dominants' status rests on their ability to gain the respect and sometimes the co-operation of others. Others attend to them, either looking towards them (as geladas) or away (as macaques) (14). A cultural innovation travels downwards more readily than it travels upward, as did the practice of washing sweet potatoes amongst Japanese macaques. Since the dominant is the one who is attended to, a creature can achieve dominance by forcing attention - as did a Gombe chimpanzee by rolling empty oil-drums around the clearing (a trick he remembered over a gap of years) (56). Where dominants do have an advantage in breeding (which is not a universal rule), the selective pressure is to produce creatures that can attract and hold the attention - a point which somewhat modifies my account of dominants as merely negative forces. There is some reason - to risk a generalization - to think that hedonic modes are more usual towards a female dominant, and agonistic towards a male, but this is not a universal rule (100).

Relationships are complicated by the fact that submission is signalled both by infantile behaviour and also by female behaviour. Amongst animals that maintain individual territories, at least during the breeding season, potential mates signal their readiness, and inhibit the male's display, by presenting themselves. Subordinate males, in hierarchical kinds, also present, and the dominant male usually signals his status by mounting. Female subordinates (at least among birds) sometimes turn out to be male, when the alpha bird is removed (whether because the observer made a mistake, or because of glandular changes). It is therefore usual for ethologists to describe the females as subordinate to the dominant male, and to infer that male dominance is a fact of life (except in quite exceptional species like the jacana). But this is not a valid inference. The dominant male may be accorded some respect, but so may the senior females. Females may forestall aggression by ritual submission: it does not follow that they are enthralled. Rather the dominance rituals linking possibly-competing males allow subordinates to play the part of females (usually), and so elicit behaviour and emotions different from those owed to rivals. Dominance-mounting and sexual-mounting do not mean the same thing; which is a metaphor for the other, as it were, can only be learnt in individual cases. Is the dominant proclaiming his mastery of the female, or is he expressing (creating?) an affection for the male? The fact that male monkeys acquire erections when considering the young suggests, in view of their general attitude and (also) of human introspection, that they are *fond* of them, not that they wish to threaten them (102). But cases differ.

A genuinely social group of individuals who can recognize each other and exercise at any rate a limited foresight is likely to be structured in many ways. These include the following dimensions: dominance, the parent-infant bond, the sexual (56). Interestingly, these correspond, though inexactly, with the three fundamental structures of Aristotle's household: master-slave, parent-child and husband-wife. From these relationships society is made.

Or at any rate, a good deal of society is made from these, if they are suitably generalized. Not only mothers feel attracted to infants: there comes a time in the growth of infants when they are treated in another way, but for the earlier part they can expect some tolerance and care from their elders, even approaching quasi-parental concern. The sexual bond, although it does not have the force that earlier ethologists had supposed (for animals are only rarely of constant sexual interest to each other), none the less provides a low level of involvement amongst the group, a diffused sexuality that reaches its peak in human beings. The hedonic mode covers much that is libidinal in origin: grooming, and petting, and exchanging or sharing food. These activities may go on alongside the agonistic modes that are enshrined in dominance routines, or they may be blended with them if the dominants are of a gentler type. This allows for what can be called a more personal sort of bonding than the hierarchical allows: two animals divided in the hierarchy may yet be friends, although (when occasion strikes) one dominates the other. Roles change with time and season. A mother submissive to the alpha male may yet protect her child by tricking him, pretending there's an enemy about (14). Where we stand in the hierarchy is not all that matters to us; and it may not matter very much.

Dominance is not always quite the same as leadership: a good pusher, one who can acquire private resources without much effort, may not be a good puller, one who can lead the troupe away or get them doing things (60). Often it is the female who is more truly the leader: where the female is also dominant, less tension exists, so that 'matriarchies' are more stable (40). The more sophisticated the intelligence of the creatures concerned, the more possible it is for subordinates to manipulate those higher than themselves in the hierarchy. Respect for the dominants may be linked with a quite clear grasp of how to get past them. This feature of social life has its place in human society also.

Dominance and the supernormal

But human dominants have greater resources than our cousins do. At a local level, in the small groups for which we are evolved, doubtless little else is needed than the dignified gaze and attractive display of other primates, but in larger societies there is need for greater display, and even in the local groups some deviant forms (as patriarchy) need considerable backing-up. In this context we need to consider the supernormal stimulus (95).

The oyster-catcher (or some oyster-catchers) can be conned into sitting on a model egg many sizes too large to be (in our eyes) a convincing replica of her own eggs. Oyster-catchers clearly like really large eggs, and are presumably not very disappointed that they do not hatch. Similar desires lie behind the cuckoo's success. The egg offers a supernormal stimulus: that is, some artificial shapes and patterns are more effective than the natural ones, the ones that are in fact associated with the evolutionary functions for which there has been selection. Evolution does not equip us with exact powers of recognition: the oyster-catcher does not need to discriminate eggs that are exactly in the right range, for there is in general no danger (in the absence of psychologists) that any too-large eggs will come her way. In general, the larger the egg the better. The sweetness of sugar is, for similar reasons, a supernormal stimulus for us (65). In the wild there was no danger we would get too much.

Applying this lesson to those cues which elicit deference: we are naturally impressed by height, and wide shoulders, measured tread and gaze. So human dominants wear head-dress, sit on thrones, look stern and stately in their robes and feathers (31). And since what cues our deference may be a relatively schematic pattern, not the concrete individual, we can even elicit deference by symbols: robins fight red feathers. Some symbolism, of the sort we share with other primates, is most probably innate, though it would be difficult (not to say wicked) to devise control experiments to prove the point. Others are artificial, acquired by virtue of our kind's readiness to pick up such things, and maybe resting on the common experience of early infancy, or else on purely inventive skills.

Whether innate or not, our symbols play the part of releasing mechanisms, and have given our dominants an enormous advantage. A hamadryas baboon needs to be around to stake his claim upon 'his' females: not that he must always be struggling to retain them, for his fellows do respect his priority, but that in his absence, or out of sight, that respect wears thin. There is nothing to stop other males trying their luck, for there is nothing to remind them that they are not merely lustful males, but also (as it were) trespassing on another's territory. It is possible to interpret things differently, to suggest that the baboons perform an intelligent calculation of risk and come to the conclusion that it is only worth trying for the females whom another male will seek to segregate when that male is out of sight. Commentators who wish to denigrate baboons are divided: calculation shows a prudent intelligence, immediate (though localized) respect offers an analogy with human morals. In fact, both mechanisms may be at work, in us and in baboons.

Where respect can be elicited in the absence of any concrete individual by a schematized representation of the sort of individuals who require and get respect, the morality of our kind can begin. There is all the difference between the sort of taboo that can be laid down by concrete individuals in their own presence, and one that floats free of all concrete backing. Sometimes such taboos are conceived simply as barriers, to be respected without further reasoning; sometimes as the prohibitions of a god, who is imagined with the character of dominant or very attractive human beings - but much more so. Whether beasts entertain such fantasies - I imply nothing about their truth or lack of it – we do not know, though it seems possible that our success in domesticating dogs may rest upon their readiness to find a supernormal stimulus in us: men serve as super pack-leaders (28). Badgers, by contrast, are not fully domesticable, lacking that disposition to submit to rule (31).

Creatures who can and do defer to relatively abstract forms as well as to concrete individuals can feel themselves subject to these forms wherever they are. A morality that rests on something more than a personal response to individual conspecifics offers both advantages and dangers. The danger is that in our deference to abstract norms we may forget the concrete individuals whose lives we share. The advantage is that social groups need not be restricted to those few creatures whom we can recognize as individuals. Human societies are not bound together solely by personal attachments of affection and deference: anyone, whether personally known to us or not, who carries the appropriate symbol is to be treated in such and such a way.

The humanistic ideal of treating all men equally may rest on this: providing all men with the symbols which elicit respect for dominants. Two possible analogies suggest themselves. On the one hand, rats: not that rats treat all rats equally – strange rats are not treated well – but they treat all rats with the right smell equally, and the strange rat who is torn to pieces seems almost to acquiesce (at any rate, does not fight back as against a predator) (64). But rats do not appear to recognize each other as individuals at all: any sweet-smelling rat will do. Humanists love the smell (metaphorical, maybe) of humanity, but must also deal with the existence of personal attachments.

On the other hand, territorial behaviour itself: where each creature (or each lucky creature) has an area of land to defend, no absolute hierarchy exists. Even the weakest land-owner has an area to lord it over. From this root stems anarchic individualism, an unwillingness to submit to general rule, conjoined with readiness to respect each other's domain. This system too does not require any personal recognition, merely the appropriate symbolism.

Neither of these systems quite accommodates what human systems of morality require: a junction of personal attachment and deference and of relatively impersonal respect for creatures we do not know or who cannot elicit respect by their own qualities. Whatever moral principles we eventually accept, it may historically be right to say that human moralism begins with respect for the relatively abstract forms

enshrined in deities. The respect we pay our fellows was owed
not to them, in virtue of their being dominant, or infantile, or
sexually attractive, but to the god, the super-dominant who
kept all lesser leaders in their place. Our image of a jealous
and protective god is drawn from our evolutionary past: the
shining figure (mother or male 'mother') who protects the
defenceless against aggressive males, or against predators, and
of whom we had better be careful. How far this god's
protection stretches is another matter: all the tribe, or all of
humankind, or every living creature? God-fearing societies can
certainly be as exclusive in their actions as are rats.

By this account, humanistic morality emerges from the
deference patterns known amongst social animals who share an
area at least for part of the year. The respect we owe our
invisible lord reinforces personal attachments and deference,
and also provides protection for those outside such personal
groupings. But of course in the absence of a visible lord people
may begin to change their attitudes: either they revert to
purely local considerations, ties of affection and immediate
deference, or else they hope to have the system of morality
without its lord. In taking the latter option we return a little
to the pattern of territorial behaviour: each owner's claim is
respected, not because anyone or anything can enforce it, but
simply as a claim.

Accordingly, there are three kinds of moralist: first, those
who acknowledge ties of friendship and submit to dominants,
but do not reckon any rule requires a universal charity or self-
restraint; second, those whose obedience to abstract order
results in something like a territorial respect for every individual's claims; thirdly, those who owe obedience to an abstract
and invisible super-dominant who enjoins good order upon all
creatures.

Chapter 10

MORAL ARGUMENT

Sociobiology and ethics

As higher mammals we are likely to find it relatively easy to form or enter into local attachments of affection and deference. We are likely to be concerned for infants, to wish to fit in with our fellows, male and female, to defer to dominants (and to the aged, within limits). Rape, murder, theft are likely to be (relatively) rare within small communities uncontaminated by patriarchalism. This is not to say that higher mammals always behave just as the higher morality would demand: we are also likely to be unconcerned for (even hostile towards) strangers, to be ready to let the weakened starve, to react to obvious disease in others by ostracising them (as the Gombe chimpanzees did a polio-stricken group-member) (58). None the less it is not unusual for those who have lived with and watched a group of beasts to conclude that they are loyal, protective and affectionate towards each other. They show behaviour that, if they were human, few would hesitate to call courageous, courteous or motherly. They are also irritable, demanding, and sometimes cruel. It is hardly surprising that so many moralists have found moral lessons in our cousins' behaviour, either as example or as horrid warning.

That these behaviour patterns can be explained in evolutionary terms does not show that they are not virtuous or vicious. That altruism offers an evolutionary 'advantage' to the agent goes no way to showing that the agent is not genuinely altruistic (even if the altruism is not universal). But it may well be that the complexities of human moralizing so far transcend anything that we can see in beasts as to make the comparison of only limited value. Humanists have rightly observed that recent efforts to equate human bars on 'incest' with the general unwillingness of females to mate with their brothers wholly ignore the subtleties of what counts as 'incest' among different human tribes (77). The usual two schools of thought contend: on the one hand, those who think that non-human behaviour is of an entirely different kind from human morality; on the other, those who suggest that ethics will soon be absorbed by sociobiology (104, 105). I have very little sympathy with either side.

That beastly and human behaviour are entirely different I find incredible. Many of our attitudes of deference and con cern seem so much of a piece with those of our kindred that they are likely to be innate, or else very easily learnt. We share them with our fellow primates. Other features of our lives may be evolved as analogues to other mechanisms that determine other animals: whatever causes ants to sacrifice themselves is probably (not certainly) rather different from human altruism, and even if it is not it is unlikely to be something that we and ants retain from our common ancestors of umpteen million years ago. Fish, ichthyosaurs and cetaceans have evolved much the same method of swimming through the sea: but not all sea-creatures travel just like that, nor have all just the same shape and habits. All social creatures, similarly, may have a common problem, but not all their problems will be in common, and not all their solutions. The more distant of our kindred are reminders of how variously social, and even (within their limits) intelligent, kinds can live. Our closer relatives, who share so many of our problems, share our solutions not merely because they are solutions, but because we have close common ancestors.

That we are primates may well impose limits on the sort of solutions we could adopt, at least without massive efforts of social control and genetic engineering. We will never live like rats, let alone bees, until our descendants have entirely outgrown their heritage. A recent report that East African mole-rats have a social structure paralleling that of the social insects (single fertile female, sterile female workers and male drones) suggests that even mammals can develop in ways that seem thoroughly unmammalian! The case is a problem for evolutionary theorists, but need not seem too threatening to moralists (51). Other proposed solutions we could adopt, but could not sustain: total celibacy for all would be an evolutionary cul-de-sac. There have been those who have contended that universal altruism must be so too. Does the evolutionary perspective give us reason to expect that ethics will be swallowed up by sociobiology?

Those scientists who have asserted this would be more convincing if their notion of ethics was not so jejune. Anyone who can suppose that ethical argument and debate is a matter of consulting one's limbic system (104) clearly does not know what it is that sociobiology is to take over. Can some argument be devised to warrant biological imperialism?

The claim, presumably, must run as follows. We have the innate attitudes and responsiveness that we have, and we easily acquire what habits are easily acquired, because they are the ones which did, in practice, lead to our development. They worked 'better', from the point of view of evolutionary advantage, than whatever rivals were on offer. We can there-fore treat our habits, dispositions, attitudes as if they were calculated means towards the propagation of our own genetic line. Now the point about something valued as a means is that it must, rationally, be abandoned or changed when there is good reason to think that it does not serve the end for which it was valued, or does not do so as well as some other option. Accordingly, we should direct our attention to the goal of preserving our genetic line, and approach sociobiologists (and computer experts) for a games-theory calculation of the best options. Ethical enquiry will become an easily calculable affair, and what is right and wrong for us to do will be read from the computer print-out. Another 'art' will be displaced by objective calculation, requiring no judgement, wisdom or good will, but only access to a computer.

I do not see that any other argument will do the job. It certainly seems to be implicit in a good deal of sociobiological writing that all individuals *should* so act as to maximize the probability of their own genes' appearing in a higher proportion of the next generation than they do in their own. The older claim that 'species-survival' was the ultimate value has lapsed in favour of more local concerns: 'the selfish gene' cares nothing for species-survival, only for its own (24). But it should surely be obvious that the argument is broken-backed, and to point this out should be a job for any competent editor, let alone a philosopher. Even if we accept, which we need not, that our attitudes have been selected as the 'fittest' for their sometime environment, it does not follow that they should be regarded as of value only in so far as they are still the 'fittest'. They are not calculated means to ends, even if they have in the past served some evolutionary function. To suppose that we are now bound or obligated to take our own genetic success as the supreme value in ethical enquiry displays the endemic confusion of function and goal to which I have referred before. That we should have children, or more generally creatures that resemble us, to survive us, does matter to some, even most, of us. But so do other things. Our normal moralizing does not treat everything as a means to our genetic success, and sociobiology gives us no reason to make such a revolutionary shift.

Moral scepticism

It may seem, however, that if we have the values that we do solely because it has 'paid' our ancestors to have them, our own conviction must be weakened. Other species, wakening to self-awareness, might find that they valued quite other things than we. If we only value what we do because we happen to have evolved that way, it may seem quite as disquieting as the discovery that we value what we do only because we were brought up to do so. What might we reasonably conclude from this (72)?

Either there is such a thing as the objectively right thing to value, or there is not. If there is not, then we may retort simply that we value some things, even if other creatures would not: none of us is strictly mistaken, for there is nothing to be mistaken about. We only have different tastes, and so will work for different worlds. Temperaments may differ here: some will find no difficulty in retaining their innocent devotion to what they happen to value, while recognizing that they are not *right* to value it, that they would not be *wrong* if they changed their goals. Others may find that they can no longer be quite so dedicated: does it matter, in any ultimate sense, what happens in the world? Well it matters to us, but how much does it matter if we can no longer back our devotion by the thought that we are doing what is *right*?

Scepticism about the objectivity of morals (68) may lead to a lessening of moral concern. Indeed, I think it is almost bound to do so. But it does not remove the possibility of deciding what is to be done in a more or less rational manner. We may not mind quite so much what is done, but we do have preferences. We can discover what we as individuals prefer, and what system of decision-making can be negotiated between those whose wishes we must take into account. We do not risk doing things objectively wrong, but we may be risking outcomes that we would rather (on consideration) not.

What if there are objective values, things we ought to value and would be wrong if we did not? Does an evolutionary account of how we come to recognize them throw doubt on our accuracy? Well, why should it? An evolutionary account could (in principle) be given of how we come to perceive things in the world (trees, lions, people) as we do: does it follow that we see them wrongly, or that they are not there to be seen? How we come to have a belief is a quite different question from whether that belief is true or false. None the less, although our belief might be accurate it would hardly be justified if we have it because of some feature which has no connection with its *truth*. I am justified in believing that this is a typewriter because part of what has caused me to have this belief is the fact that it is a typewriter. If there were no typewriter here some quite different causal story would have to be told to explain my having this belief. If there were a typewriter here, but I believed this because I was hypnotized into doing so (and would believe it even if there weren't), my belief would not be justified, even though it were correct. How does this touch the status of our values, what we value?

If part of what has caused me to have the innate modes of factual discrimination that I do (substances, motions, causes, colours etc.) is the fact that there are such things in the world (and creatures who failed to see things so did not survive), then my beliefs in the matter are both accurate and justified. I am justified in believing that fire burns because it does, and because I believe it because it does (though this account needs to be modified to accommodate justified beliefs that happen to be false). Without such a causal link between the fact and my belief, my belief is not justified, and if I come to believe that my beliefs are not so caused I can no longer claim that they are justified, that I am justified in holding them. If rational, I would cease to believe them (or believe them less).

I shall not now consider the alarming argument that our factual beliefs are caused not by the facts of the case but by the profitability (genetic and personal) of having those beliefs. By this account our factual beliefs are all unjustified (including, obviously, this account). But epistemology is too large a topic to advance upon (18). Let me instead consider only the ethical dimension. If there are objective values, do we have the beliefs we do about them because they are what we think? Is there the same constraint upon the formation of ethical beliefs that there is (or may seem to be) upon factual, that those creatures who tend to get it wrong do not leave progeny?

To this there seem to me to be three answers: yes, and yes, and no.

The negative answer first: creatures who fail to reckon that fire burns, that poisonous frogs are poisonous, that hawks can kill, do not as a rule leave progeny. We are constantly compelled to get things right. But creatures who fail to perceive objective values correctly may breed as well as any. Such values are not items in the world against which we stub our toes. The objective rightness of a course of action or the real value of something that we value does not seem to enter into the evolutionary tale at all. That it pays an individual to act so, or that it 'pays' a kind that individuals should act so, is not the same as the objective rightness of the act. If we have the values that we do solely because it 'paid' our ancestors, we do not have them because they are correct: accordingly we are not justified in thinking that we have got them right, and we must (if rational) abandon them as serious attempts to speak the truth. Whether we continue to believe that objective value is accessible at all, or if it is not what manner of use it may be, are other questions. In practice an inaccessible objective value is no value at all (1 (*Nicomachean Ethics* 1.6)): this option ends in the same place as moral scepticism. If such values are accessible somehow, by special revelation, we abandon this world's ways for a transcendent world's.

The first positive answer seems to be that of some biologists: if our beliefs about objective values are to be justified they must have been caused in us by those same values. Since what causes us to be born having or easily acquiring those beliefs is the power of neo-Darwinian selection, let us equate 'objective value' with evolutionary success. The objective test of ethical beliefs is simply: Does it 'pay'? If being objectively valuable were a matter of being 'successful' we should have a test of objective value, and should be justified in holding at least the firmest and most nearly innate of our own attitudes: so let us say that it is. This *tour de force* convinces few philosophers. If 'objective value' consists in such 'success', so much the worse for objective value. Such a radical suggestion, that we should above all admire and work for such evolutionary 'success', cannot be rendered plausible merely by pretending that it is a tautology, that objective value simply is survival value. If it makes sense to ask after objective value at all (and that is a topic which I do not here consider), it makes sense to ask whether it is objectively valuable that a given kind, or given gene, be 'successful'. Evolutionary success can only be contingently related to ethical accuracy: that we have certain attitudes may show that the having of them brought some 'advantage' to our ancestors - it does not of itself show that they are correct.

The third answer agrees with the second that we have the values that we do in part because those values are what they are, and also that we have such values because we have evolved to have them. The answer is that it is because objective value is what it is that we have been evolved as we have, that the world is so constituted that creatures of our kind are likely to evolve. Objective value does not enter into the evolutionary story at the historical level: it is not because creatures are doing what is objectively right that they survive and have descendants, but because their natural traits increase their inclusive genetic fitness. But it is possible that the whole natural system has been made in such a way that evolutionary logic will lead to creatures of a moral kind. We have the beliefs we do because we have evolved to have them; we have evolved to have them because the values we admire were themselves operative in establishing the whole evolutionary process. We are justified in our beliefs because the truth of those beliefs plays a part in establishing the system that brings about those beliefs. Value, in short, is creative. The name tradition gives to this creative value is God: the supernormal stimulus we fantasize has real existence and brought all our world to be. To investigate natural law is to discover more of God's nature (but it need not be that everything in Nature is God's handiwork).

This last solution has the further merit of providing some content to the notion of objective value: although some philosophers still suspect that there are such values (the values, for example, of honesty and logical thought), which are more than our agreements to behave in certain ways, it has proved difficult to say what their mode of being might be. The theological moralist can locate them as the character and commands of God, not as Platonic forms existing independently of all valuations. But the ramifications of theological morality would take me too far afield.

Moral systems

Objectivists are doomed to moral scepticism, to some gnostic transcendentalism or to theism. Which of these, if any, is correct is not a matter for sociobiology, but for metaphysicians of morals. Maybe moral theses are merely expressive of our preferences and prescriptions; maybe they report objective truths which our evolution has somehow equipped us to see. One thing they clearly are not is the inarguable expression of mood, as though moral debate were only an exchange of ejaculations. Our deference towards established authority, our affection for the young, our unwillingness to slaughter clan-mates, may issue in approving or disapproving comments that can in turn be generalized. Ethical praise and dispraise leads on, in us, to argument: such and such a creature is courageous and a good parent, but bullies subordinates and casually betrays clan-mates. Is such a creature to be admired? What matters more to us? Do we help our children or our friends? When should we keep promises, or when obey the Queen? Often enough we manage no more than a conscientious determination to do this rather than that, on this occasion. We cannot give any rule to explain why *this* is right this time, any more than most of us can tell quite how we stay balanced on our bicycles. But it does not follow that our moral decisions are arbitrary, nor that they issue without reflection from our limbic system.

Moral argument

Recent moral philosophy has expended energy chiefly on attempts to articulate a moral theory, or set of moral principles, that we could use to decide our perplexities. Some have hoped to deduce such principles from axioms of rationality that no one could deny without radical incoherence; others have expected only that we might uncover the rules which, by and large, we follow already in our intuitive discriminations. The laws of logic, in their first discovery, are patterns found by inspecting what arguments we recognize as right in every case: if an argument of the same form can be found to generate a false conclusion from true premises then that argument is invalid. Only later are such laws incorporated in a single system, derived from supposedly self-evident axioms. The laws of ethics likewise may be established by considering what priorities we seriously have, what choices we recognize as right. Or they may at last be derived from axioms as obvious, to the wise, as are the axioms of logic to those who know them.

I do not myself feel much hope of such a system. It seems to me more likely that we must rely upon our best endeavours in particular situations, on the discriminations made by well-informed and balanced characters. But even they will be assisted by seeing how the maxims implicit in particular choices would operate in other conditions, and seeing whether they would approve of them. The puzzles of the moralist are these: if it is right to save ten at the price of not saving one (supposing it impossible to save eleven), how is it not right to *kill* one to save ten (say, by organ-transplant)? What balance should we make between obedience and autonomy, pleasure and duty? How shall we organize our States, or educate our children? What obedience, if any, is owed to lawful authority? What is the importance of knowledge? Or how far should creatures' species make a difference to how we treat them? In sorting through our choices, and debating with each other, we may hope to move toward a system that accommodates our various values, that is run by laws whose implications we can bear.

The moral theories supported by some of our contemporaries are more systematic: the utilitarian and the contractual. The utilitarian directive (or directives: the thing is more complex than at first it seems) is to do that act which has the greatest probability of bringing about the greatest happiness of the greatest number (classical theory was not speciesist, though Mill allowed greater importance to distinctively human pleasures). Within that framework moralists may hope to settle particular issues, once they have determined what is to count as happiness, and whether the creatures or their contentment is to matter more (are a few very happy creatures to be preferred to many less happy creatures?). Utilitarians make no distinction between act and omission, allow no standing rights of property or autonomy to prevent the working through of the overall plan. Subspecies of the utilitarian kind dispute whether lesser rules are to be accounted rules of thumb, or as requiring action even if, on this occasion, omission would itself be more directly profitable. Are we to kill the innocent lest worse befall? Are ordinary citizens to be utilitarian, or is that status reserved for the social engineers?

Contractual theorists, on the other hand, require that we rule our lives by those rules that we would have agreed upon if we had had the chance of debating the matter without personal bias or predilection. All men (at any rate) have rights over their own persons, and no one is to be taxed or commanded save (at most) for the benefit of the worst-off members of society. Liberal and right-wing contractualists dispute concerning the State's right to interfere.

Both these theories, in their many versions, present the serious thinker with problems. Whether they are aimed as approximations to an objective moral order, or merely as articulations of our preferences (or their professors'), they can be debated and compared without recourse to sociobiology. No evidence has yet been presented that sociobiology could possibly contribute to this debate (90). Nor is it likely that non-human animals will help us here. Maybe they have their own debates, but we are not party to them. Maybe we can learn from what societies they have formed, as we can also learn from human history, but the overriding lesson of ethology, as well as history, is that living creatures are enormously variable, that no one way has seemed to suit all creatures all the time.

Beasts, so far as we can tell, do not draw out from their own actions any principles of action on which they can comment, from which they can gradually dissent. We can meditate upon the affections and fears we find ourselves feeling. We can ask what we would do in such-and-such circumstances, and what difference there may be between that case and this. It is the mark of great folly not at least to aim at a sort of consistency: if we claim to be doing this action because of such-and-such a feature, but would not do, or would not even think it right to do, a similar action in a similar situation, then it cannot be because of that feature we were performing the action. Either we had no reason at all, or it was not what we thought, and maybe when we think of it we do not wholly like to act on reasons such as those. If I cannot bear to generalize my principles, do I have principles at all? Or must I not sometimes admit that only an immediate judgement is possible, that we cannot prescribe for all such situations, because we cannot be quite sure (in advance of examples) what counts as 'just the same situation'?

All these perplexities are our affair. Beasts may sometimes feel them too, but if they do, we do not know it, and it seems more likely, in general, that they do not. Beasts, let us say, are *ethical*: that is, they respond to aspects of a situation and to features of their kindred, that a good man also would respect. But they are not *moral*: for they do not, as far as we can see, have any occasion to moralize about themselves or to construct intellectual systems to accommodate their immediate responses. Moralists and philosophers may emphasize either of these aspects of the good life. For those of the rationalist tradition the moral has been supreme: what matters is to provide a coherent account of the rational principles from which we may deduce right action, irrespective of our feelings and desires. The culmination of this tradition lies in Kant: to act according to that maxim which we could will to be natural law, or which we could conceive to be binding upon any rational creatures. Acting from mere affection, fear or squeamishness is not enough. For those of the non-rationalist tradition (broadly, the empiricist), the ethical has ruled: we should act out our best synthesis of the values we are evolved to have, not expecting that any rational being would have just the same values (unless having some such value is a prerequisite for being rational) (71).

Rationalists, emphasizing the moral, are likely to find beasts wholly other than human; empiricists, like David Hume, recognize beasts as our cousins, moved by ethical concerns that move us also (50). The truth, no doubt, lies in between: a banal enough conclusion, maybe, but one worth emphasizing. Not even Kant could give his categorical imperative any content without appealing to the facts of natural sentiment; even those who found their morals upon sentiment will usually acknowledge that rational argument can sometimes show their sentiments to be ill-judged. We are unlike the beasts, or what we know of them, in this: that we have scope to see that we were wrong.

Chapter 11

CONCLUSIONS

The rules of moral discourse are not deducible from sociobiological premises. No amount of biological theorizing will answer the meta-ethical questions about the status of moral values, nor the ethical questions about what we are to do (with ourselves, with others) that I have sketched. Nor can studies of animal behaviour do more than offer us examples of what might be done. But we may still be able to learn some things of moral importance from the study of our kindred.

Every moral theory implies some view of what human beings are. Perhaps we are spiritual intellects, fallen into a world of desire and feeling that is fundamentally alien to us: it is the principles of intellect that we should honour. Perhaps we are made in the image of God, entirely other than the apes and automata that lack a soul. Perhaps we are ourselves automata, programmed to seek our survival and our profit at all costs. Perhaps we are elder siblings of the other beasts, or slaves of God, or naked apes. None of these views could be entirely disproved by any observation: it is a rare theory that cannot swallow up a 'refutation' or two. But we may at least come to find them less plausible (or more plausible) as we examine our own history and that of other creatures in the world.

My own belief is that we are mammals, and part of the flock of God: my anthropology has its roots in both biology and religion. Nothing very detailed follows from this: we cannot even extrapolate from the behaviour of a North Indian langur to that of a South Indian langur (53). But some things are expectable. We can expect that human beings will be relatively affectionate to members of their immediate circle, in particular to children. They will form groups, of both sexes and all ages, and generally restrict their sexual activity within those groups. They will range fairly widely, and will not usually erect territorial boundaries (as individuals, or pairs) in the way that birds so often do (amongst the primates, only gibbons are territorial in anything like the way birds are). Human beings will probably be inclined to defer to the more impressive of their number, not to carry violence to the extreme within their group, and sometimes to care for each other. The development of assertoric language, and of sharing, seem to be almost species-specific (106). Like other primates, they will be relatively difficult to toilet-train, but tidiness and cleanliness will not be wholly unnatural for them. All of these remarks admit of exceptions: not all human beings talk, not all are tidy; some are murderously violent, even to their children. But enough is predictable to make us doubt some of the characterizations of humanity that have come down to us.

Affection towards clan-mates, love of children, deference to authority, disinclination to kill those who have reminded us of common humanity, even some respect for property: these features of human life do not, it seems, stem from our intellectual gifts. We share them with our cousins. Certainly a human society may not display these features, or not display all of them. We are adept at distorting our own natures. But they are so far *natural* to humanity as to pose problems for our understanding when they are absent: how far can we really understand a people who defer to no one, despise the old, hate their children, use sex solely as an instrument of war, and kill anyone they get a chance to kill? The psychopath is, in a real sense, against nature (though this is not to say that an evolutionary explanation for the preservation of psychopathy might not be forthcoming).

If it is as mammals that we have this nature, or as primates, then our moral systems are enormously elaborated rationalizations of pre-rational sentiments. We cannot conclude that no moral system which denied these sentiments could be maintained, but it is doubtful whether it could be long maintained. A mammalian group which really attempted to bring up its children to regard themselves as interchangeable components, or to hate their spouses and their children, or to suppress all sexual desire except at stated intervals, would be very unlikely to succeed (unless 'favourable' mutations coincidentally occurred). But I do not imply that such mammalian groups as act out their natures will behave as moral men of our tradition would. Animal affection is very closely tied to familiars: these are amongst the strongest pressures that lead to the emergence of new species, that we like creatures of a familiar kind and are enraged by strangers. Wholly alien things, indeed, may be hated less. It is the almost-human that we see as loathly, for it is our conspecifics that are the rivals of our lines and clans. Aliens do not compete, in general, for the same resources – though humankind has made so much of the world its own resource that almost every kind now rivals us. 'Natural virtue' is not always wholly good: a creature may be an affectionate, even a devoted parent and clan-mate, but be ruthlessly opposed to strange conspecifics. It is all too easy for us to convince ourselves that such-and-such is not really 'human', but rather vermin. Conversely, we hate such things as rats when we see them as depraved humans. One disturbing report says that Washoe (the earliest of the Ameslan apes), on being introduced to chimpanzees who had not learnt American Sign Language, referred to them (with apparent hostility) as 'black bugs' (62): xenophobia, as it also seems from reports of the Gombe chimpanzees' 'wars' (32), is a habit we share with our cousins. Contempt is a mammalian pattern too.

The fact is that humankind is still one species, and that deserves an explanation. For some reason human groups have not engaged in so much inbreeding as to form new species, though some of them have been almost wholly isolated from the others for many millennia. Why can we still interbreed? Such behavioural barriers as exist, differences of sexual practice and expectation, are plainly insufficient to prevent interbreeding, and are cultural in origin, not yet embedded in the chromosomes.

Outbreeding groups, of course, obtain a slight advantage in genetic variety: this is the basis for the minimal bar against 'incest' observed amongst the beasts. But the exchange of seed (*not* 'the exchange of females') between human groups is not of a piece with that preference for males of their group other than their brothers shown by female chimpanzees. Of course some species have evolved complex adaptations in favour of outbreeding, but there is little evidence that such an innate disposition lies at the root of human intermarriage. Almost certainly this is a cultural step, relying on an innate fascination with difference, perhaps, but enforcing outbreeding against the impulse to prefer familiar mates. We are perhaps one species because our ancestors took steps to see that we would be.

Alternatively, we are the product of that problem, the surplus male, shared by most mammalian species. The young males on the fringes of the group will be the first to perish in a war; victorious males are then absorbed by the opposing female lineage (peacefully or otherwise). Men fight wars (functionally) to possess the women; women submit to conquerors (functionally) to improve the variety of their line. Their motives, obviously, are another matter (32).

These two models, of benevolent statesmanship and of the after-effects of war, need not be mutually exclusive. Both have changed our history often enough for it to be likely that they changed our prehistory as well. One further reason for taking the former model seriously is as follows.

Almost alone among animals, humans domesticate and dwell with other animals (49). So-called 'slaver ants', who rob the nests of other ant-species of their grubs, hatching them to provide the workers that this species does not breed itself, and the ordinary ants who appear to 'farm' aphids, are exceptions. But the mechanisms that are involved in these cases are unlikely to be of help in understanding the human. For many millennia human beings have had to behave as if they were concerned about the welfare of certain animals, notably dogs, cattle, sheep, horses. The easiest way for 'nature' to achieve this is for us really to be concerned. Even before we had domesticated animals, our hunting ancestors needed to feel some concern for the prey animals. Chimpanzees may grab young baboons without more than a guilty qualm or two, but they do not live on baboons. The more important game became to our ancestors, the more they had to be concerned not to over-kill their prey. When they had domesticated prey or allies they must care for the well-being of the animals. People who cared for their animals left more descendants than those who used them carelessly, and sentimental attachment or awe-struck admiration were more secure and easier ways of achieving this result than any ponderous forethought. It 'paid' to like animals, and to like them glossy and contented. It may be (we have no real evidence) that the gap between those human groups who love dogs and those who treat them as pariahs is by now genetic: the dog 'paid' Caucasians better (but maybe not) (28). In such a liking for creatures quite unlike the human form, though socialized as members of the human group (living, sleeping, working together), we may find the basis for our partial and insecure welcoming of the human or almost-human, our strange conspecifics. Some of us are 'turned off' by the strange; others are 'turned on', because it 'paid' our ancestors to love what wasn't human.

Such a love, of course, is guilty. For the animals our ancestors cared for were very often destined for the slaughter. Our ancestors had to love them, but to be ready to kill them. It is understandable that so many groups have elaborated rituals to cope with these embarrassments: displacement acti-vities, one might call them - what we do when we can't do quite what we want, because we want too many things. If I am right that care for animals and willingness to mate outside the tribe are closely connected developments, it is not surprising that animal-shapes have so often symbolized the mating-groups that human bars on incest have created. By thinking of strange humans as if they were beasts we can move toward them. E. Reed may even be right to attribute the complex of ideas in this area to benevolent matriarchs coping with their surplus males, or with the incoming males' tendency to kill and

eat the children of old males (if we were once like hanuman
langurs in this) (77). Our relations with beasts lie at the centre
of moral enquiry (17).

This is speculation, though it has its uses. What is very
probable is that our human beginnings do indeed lie in such
family groups. We did not evolve as anonymous individuals in
an amorphous herd (though like other social mammals we may
have the option of forming such herds *in extremis*); nor is it
likely that we evolved as pair-bonding creatures in a nuclear
family. Our groups were group marriages, even though 'marriage' they should not strictly be called until the full development of a contractual and symbolizing system. The human and
prehuman family was not composed of a man, a woman and
their offspring. That family was one of mothers and daughters
and such males as were acceptable. We in the West have grown
a long way from that pattern, but it is worth remembering still
(22, 102). Those who dislike the closed nuclear family can win
ammunition from ethology (19).

The mutual grooming of the primate horde and other
hedonic linkages between individuals also provide us with a
model for society, and incidentally for sexuality, other than
the right-wing insistence on peck-orders and sexual dimorph-
ism. Instead of expecting human societies to fall into hierarchical and sexist patterns, we can identify friendship as the
central theme of the primate biogram. Homosexuals do not,
after all, present any special problem to evolutionary genetics
(how is it that they have not long ago been bred out of the
race?): all primates are likely to enjoy each other's company
and physical attentions. What is surprising, and needs (cultural)
explanation, is the lack of such close physical contact between
straight, Western males. What needs remembering also is the
extent to which dominance rituals can get in the way of open,
hedonic modes of relationship. In short, there is no need for
either Gay Lib or Women's Lib to be afraid of ethology, no
need to invent spurious rationalizations for claiming a radical
distinction between human beings and animals.

We can expect that human beings will generally be happy
in a group of both sexes, many ages and many species. They
will be intrigued and irritated, both at once, by other groups;
they will be torn by disparate emotions, love and hate, and
deference and contempt. To accommodate their tensions they
will devise shared rituals, which then may serve to mediate
relationships with groups for whom they feel no instant
empathy. Their society will be tied together not only by
affection at a local level, but by shared meanings, contracts,

Conclusions

and at last (perhaps) by prudent foresight or by force. An obvious enough conclusion, unless we have read too much political philosophy.

If that is how we stand some chance of being happy, of getting what we are likely to want, it does not follow at once that we should aim for such a society. Nor indeed does the programme offer much detail: not enough to decide, for example, how much of deference a happy society will expect from its members. But even if such enquiries did offer a detailed prospectus of a happy human society, we might still reasonably ask 'But *ought* we to strive to be happy?' For such moralists as think that moralizing is nothing but the proper ordering of our preferences, the question may make no sense (72). To say that such-and-such will make everybody happy, will give all or nearly all of us what we want, is to offer the strongest recommendation we could imagine. What on earth could count against it? A moralist for whom morality is an objective system must still have doubts: only the Good, or else the Will of God, could truly oblige us, and human happiness on its own is no more a moral end than the happiness of psychopaths (if they are happy), or of cockroaches.

To this final doubt the ethologist can give no answer. But if we take it as read that our life is, or can be, good, then the ethologist and anthropologist can contribute to the study of how best to organize our lives so as to satisfy the wants and desires that have been programmed into us, which we can ignore or subvert only at our grave peril. Such study gives us reason to believe that decency is not wholly artificial, that it needs no whips to secure its growth. But we must also remember just how easily our natural impulses may outrun prudence or a wider code of law than is provided in the family.

I have urged the advantages of an Aristotelian philosophy of science, and also of an Aristotelian meta-ethics. Aristotelian ethics are not proved by ethological data, but neither are they disproved: they remain very plausible. Moral virtue grows in one who has been brought up well, in accordance with nature, allowing scope for such affections and concerns as are part of our heritage. Such virtue involves a balance of opposite tendencies and emotions, a capacity to respond in various ways when occasion calls. There is no general pastime of humanity in which it is always wrong to indulge: the virtuous are not one-sided (16).

> For everything its season, and for every activity under heaven its time: a time to be born and a time to die; a time to plant and a time to uproot; a time to kill and a time to heal; a time to build up and a time to pull down; a

> time to weep and a time to laugh; a time for mourning
> and a time for dancing; a time to scatter stones and a
> time to gather them; a time to embrace and a time to
> refrain from embracing; a time to seek and a time to lose;
> a time to keep and a time to throw away; a time to tear
> and a time to mend; a time for silence and a time for
> speech; a time to love and a time to hate; a time for war
> and a time for peace. (Ecclesiastes 3.1-8)

Having no rooted obsession with one of these activities the
virtuous can see when either may be required, balancing one
claim against another, assigning each its due. How this is done
there is no rule to say.

Human beings are sociable by nature: they are not forced
by fear to join together in communities. We are born into
community, and find ourselves just as we find our friends.
Surplus males, maybe, have sometimes had to hunt out other
groups to join, but even they would not have preferred to live
alone. For other species that may be a general option: the
wilfully solitary human is, for Aristotle, either a beast or a
god. In this, it seems to me, Aristotle is more realistic than
those theorists who have imagined that our society rests upon
the freely made association of adult humans. Fortunately we
have not needed to make such novel arrangements. We do not
need to be scared or bullied into staying together and co-
operating: we have families and friends.

But was Aristotle right to think that human beings were
naturally *political* animals? Is it their nature to live in a *polis*,
a city-state on the Greek model? He knew, of course, that
many human beings did not so live, but reckoned this as a
failure to achieve the form of community life that best
fulfilled human nature. Only in such a State could adult males
realize their capacity for personal and political decision-
making: for Aristotle, as for many theorists since, only free
males were genuinely human, and their humanity was realized
outside the household, in willed obedience to the Law.

The Greek city was, for its inmates, worshipful: that is, it
demanded loyalty as the embodiment of shared value. It came
to be, endowed with all the supernormal panoply of divinity, in
opposition to the clans and families which were its constitu-
ents. Aristocratic fear of anarchy notwithstanding, the Greek
city was, by modern liberal standards, totalitarian. A nation or
a mercantile association differed from a city just in that such
societies did not concern themselves with the virtue or vice of
their subjects. Cities were constructed and maintained to train
men up in the way that they should go: their justification, for
Aristotle, was that they gave those capable of such activity a

chance to help organize their lives, and to an even smaller number leisure to theorize.

My feminist reservations about this account will be obvious. It is the mothers who are the true centre of a human community, and there is no evidence worth taking seriously that women are less capable even of abstract thought (supposing that to be the essence) than are their sons and brothers. As an instrument of patriarchalism the Greek *polis* had best stay buried. But it is worth reforming. Aristotle envisages a form of society that stretches further than even an extended family, bound together by friendships and shared assumptions and admiration for the continuing presence embodied in successive generations of decision-makers. It is a form of society that we have lost. We have no genuine opportunity to direct the growth and maintenance of the community within which we find our being; we are expected to feel a sense of community with people that we have not seen, to a degree that may exceed our relatively restricted altruism (or may not); expected to help pay for schemes that we may reckon ill-advised or wicked. Liberal States permit their citizens to leave - but there is nowhere to go beyond the reach of State power in one form or another.

Old-fashioned liberals, or libertarians, may wish the abdication of the State in favour of free individuals, but have not taken seriously the problem Aristotle posed: how shall people be brought up to be the sort of people who are needed to sustain a community of the kind preferred? Libertarians have an interest in seeing that children are reared to perpetuate the ideal, liberal community: how then can they permit perfect liberty to parents to bring up their children any way they please? If we are not to relapse upon the tender cruelties of a Mister Big, our society must feel some mutual affections, a sense of community and shared value: it is on such sentiments that left-wing anarchists rely. How are children to be brought up to this? We cannot expect people to have any shared moral values unless they are brought up in a genuine community whose members care whether they do or not.

Aristotelian political theory, suitably informed by ethological data concerning the likely bases of ethical sentiment, may offer us a route between the advocates of State power in its modern form and individualistic libertarians. The social form that best fulfils our natures will be a relatively small community in which many ages, types and species are represented and in which everyone is encouraged to participate in serious decision-making. It is unlikely that any such community would long accept the favourite liberal dogma, that all rational adults are entitled to do what they please so long as they directly harm no one else.

A world made up of such communities would not be paradise, but it is doubtless Utopian. Officers of the State are unlikely to preside over its demise – and certainly not the right-wing ideologues who profess to be opposed to centralized government, while simultaneously multiplying that government's power to commit mass murder (a power paid for with money contributed willy-nilly for the services of the State) and destroying private businesses. But times may change: theorists have sometimes mocked at Aristotle for exalting the Greek city-state in the very century in which its real power was lost to empires: but the *polis* lasted longer than Alexander's gimcrack empire. Friends, families, clubs, colleges may yet outlast the State, and retrieve or create a social form with more opportunity for human excellence than is provided by the nation-state. Despite E. O. Wilson's claims, neither ethology nor anthropology nor sociobiology has shown that anarchism is unworkable (105), though of course it may be.

The still more radical alternative is to suppose that human beings are evolved to live as hunter-gatherers, in small bands, without any of the specious barriers that make us think we are unlike the other animals, do not live in the natural world. If this is so, only a catastrophe could leave our few descendants free to try again at this. If we survive in any greater numbers we are doomed to agriculture and to industry, and can reasonably hope that we are well enough adapted to some forms of these activities. In this area comparisons with hunter-gatherers or other primates will not help us much: but much of our activity will still be comprehensible, familiar to them. Wherever we go we will retain many of the same problems, and should at least consider the solutions that our kindred have found pragmatically.

The Aristotelian ethic can be interpreted as a purely naturalistic one, a way of sorting through our preferences and priorities so as to achieve a life of human happiness within a community. But for Aristotle the supreme value, the one thing that we must get right if anything is to go right, is the worship and service of God. The good city exists to provide not merely chances for decision-making, but chances for the contemplation of the divine. The truly virtuous man acts for the sake of the noble, to reflect a little of that ordered beauty that the world desires. It is because God exists as the supreme objective value that Aristotelian ethics are not only the subjective (and inevitably variable) working-through of natural preferences. It is the will of the virtuous and wise to see as God sees, and to see God reflected in the beautiful and good (16, 72).

Once a transcendent God enters the picture it becomes possible to think that even our natural valuations can fall under judgement. One strand in Aristotelian thought proclaims the wise man as the standard of what is true, as well as of what is good - to be true or good just is to be asserted or valued by the good and wise man. But the objectivist strand is there as well: that things are true or good independently of what even the wise man says. Aristotle believed that the world was such that we could get things right by our own moral and intellectual endeavour, but he also allowed that illumination was, in a sense, a thing that came from beyond. If so, perhaps the light from beyond may cast all our dogmas into doubt.

Are the morals of nature what we should adopt? The natural habits bred in us are likely to involve a greater love for kinsfolk and for friends than for a passing stranger. We are likely to care for cattle and children, but only to a point. We are likely to claim things for ourselves, and be aggrieved that they are taken from us. The virtues of the heathen are but splendid vices - or so, at any rate, it may be said. The naturalist is confronted not only by the gnostic moralist, who raises the uncomfortable question, 'Should the enterprise of earthly life go on at all?', but even by the more orthodox theist, who acknowledges the worth of natural life. The gnostic (and some Buddhists) may insist that earthly life is only a poor substitute for our real life, that the best option is to give it up. Even the more conventional believer may suggest that it is a preparation for another life, and that we should extend our concern in quite unnatural ways.

> If you love only those who love you, what credit is that to you? Even sinners love those who love them . . . But you must love your enemies and do good; and lend without expecting any return; and you will have a rich reward: you will be sons of the Most High, because he himself is kind to the ungrateful and wicked. (Luke 6.32-5)

Such a demand is that of a supernormal fantasy, or the requirement on us of a life not of this world (69). Pure gnosticism is self-cancelling: if all our natural impulse was astray how could we ever get to recognize the fact? Theists can say that we, our ancestors, have been led to the point where we can recognize, even if we cannot wholly live by, a transcendent demand. We are, in the jargon, 'pre-adapted' to a novel role.

Our morality must in the end depend not only on what we

think we are, but on what we think the world is. This question is not ethological. But though the study of our kindred's behaviour, or our own, cannot answer it, we may at least begin to understand ourselves (human and non-human) just a little better. Maybe we and all our cousins are the creatures, slaves or friends of God. In either case, the ways of beasts may set us good examples, and when we know some of the causes of our wanderings we may sometimes be free to start again.

SELECT BIBLIOGRAPHY
and
INDEX OF AUTHORS

1 Aristotle, **Basic Works,** ed. R. McKeon. Random House: New York 1941. Referred to on pp. 8, 18, 103

2 Barash, D. P., **Sociobiology and Behaviour.** Elsevier: Amsterdam 1977. 55, 67, 79, 81

3 Barnett, S. A., **Instinct and Intelligence.** MacGibbon & Kee: London 1967. 23

4 Bateson, P. P. G., and Hinde, R. A. (eds), **Growing Points in Ethology.** Cambridge University Press 1976.

5 Bedran, B. C. R., 'The Social Life of Lions', **Scientific American** 232.1975 (5) pp. 54ff. 74

6 Bernstein, I. S., 'An Investigation of the Organization of Pigtail Monkey Groups through the Use of Challenges', **Primates** 7.1966 pp. 471ff.

7 Bischoff, N., 'Comparative Ethology of Incest Avoidance', pp. 37ff. in Fox (1975). 72, 74, 75

8 Bischoff, N., 'On the Phylogeny of Human Morality', pp. 53ff. in Stent (1978). 23, 53

9 Boyle, J. M., Grisez, G. G., and Tollensen, O., **Free Choice: A Self-Referential Argument.** University of Notre Dame: Notre Dame/London 1976. 40

10 Brown, J. L., 'Alternative Routes to Sociality in Jays', **American Zoologist** 14.1974 pp. 63ff. 50

11 Bygoff, J. D., 'Cannibalism among Wild Chimpanzees', **Nature** 238.1972 pp. 410f. 35

12 Calhoun, J. B., 'Behavioral Sink', pp. 259ff. in E. B. Bliss (ed.), **Roots of Behavior.** Harper-Hoeber: New York 1962. 67

13 Caplan, A. L. (ed.), **The Sociobiology Debate.** Harper: New York 1978. 5

14 Chance, M. R. R., 'Social Cohesion and the Structure of Attention', pp. 93ff. in Fox (1975). 91f., 94

15 Cherfas, J., 'Voices in the Wilderness', **New Scientist** 86.1980 pp. 303ff. 49

16 Clark, S. R. L., **Aristotle's Man.** Clarendon Press: Oxford 1975. 31, 48, 113, 117

17 Clark, S. R. L., **The Moral Status of Animals.** Clarendon Press: Oxford 1977. 2, 112

18 Clark, S. R. L., **From Athens to Jerusalem.** Clarendon Press: Oxford (forthcoming). 2, 17, 22, 102

19 Clark, S. R. L., 'Sexual Ontology and the Group Mar-
    riage', **Philosophy** 58.1983 pp. 215ff. 77, 112
20 Clark, S. R. L., 'Awareness and Self-Awareness',
    pp. 11ff. in D. G. M. Wood-Gush, M. Dawkins and R.
    Ewbank (eds), **Awareness in Self-Domesticated Animals.**
    UFAW: Potters Bar 1981. 44
21 Clutton-Brock, T. H., and Harvey, P. D. (eds), **Readings
    in Sociobiology.** Freeman: Reading 1978.
22 Count, E. W., 'The Biological Basis for Human Society',
    American Anthropologist 60.1958 pp. 1049ff. 88, 112
23 Crook, J. H., 'Sources of Cooperation in Animals and
    Men', pp. 257ff. in Eisenberg and Dillon (1971). 80, 86
24 Dawkins, R., **The Selfish Gene.** Clarendon Press: Oxford
    1976. 10, 57, 86, 100
25 Devore, I. (ed.), **Primate Behavior.** Holt, Rinehart and
    Winston: New York 1965.
26 Dilger, W. C., 'The Behavior of Lovebirds', **Scientific
    American** 206.1962 (1) pp. 88ff. 4, 80
27 Douglas-Hamilton, I. and O., **Among the Elephants.**
    Collins: London 1975. 53
28 Downs, J. F., 'Domestication: An Examination of the
    Changing Social Relationships between Men and Ani-
    mals', **Kroeber Anthropological Society Papers** 22.1960
    pp. 18ff. 96, 111
29 Efron, R., 'Biology without Consciousness', pp. 209–34 in
    R. G. Colodny (ed.), **Logic, Laws and Life.** Pittsburgh
    University Press 1977. 14, 27
30 Ehrenfeld, D., **The Arrogance of Humanism.** Oxford Uni-
    versity Press: New York 1978. 21
31 Eibl-Eibesfeldt, I., **Love and Hate,** tr. G. Strachan. Meth-
    uen: London 1971. 6, 32, 95f.
32 Eibl-Eibesfeldt, I., **The Biology of Peace and War,** tr. E.
    Mosbacher. Thames and Hudson: London 1979. 35, 50,
    88, 110
33 Eisenberg, J. F., and Dillon, W. S. (eds), **Man and Beast:
    Comparative Social Behavior.** Smithsonian: Washington
    1971. 37, 63, 80, 83, 86, 89f.
34 Elster, J., **Ulysses and the Sirens.** Cambridge University
    Press 1979. 51
35 Etkin, W., and Freedman, D. G., **Social Behavior from
    Fish to Man.** University of Chicago Press 1967. 32
36 Eysenck, H. J., 'The Biology of Morality', pp. 108ff. in
    T. Lickona (ed.), **Moral Development and Behavior:
    Theory, Research, and Social Issues.** Holt, Rinehart and
    Winston: New York 1976. 42

37 Fox, R., 'Primate Kin and Human Kinship', pp. 10ff. in Fox (1975). 73

38 Fox, R., (ed.), **Biosocial Anthropology.** Maleby Press: London 1975. 73ff., 91f., 94

39 Frey, R. G., **Interests and Rights: The Case Against Animals.** Oxford University Press 1980. 24

40 Fromm, E., **The Anatomy of Human Destructiveness.** Cape: London 1974. 33, 72, 94

41 Gillan, D., Premack, D., and Woodruff, G., 'Animal Behavior Processes', **Journal of Experimental Psychology** 7.1981 pp. 1ff. 33

42 Goody, J., **The Domestication of the Savage Mind.** Cambridge University Press 1977. 31

43 Griffin, D. R., **The Question of Animal Awareness.** Rockefeller University Press 1976. 28

44 Hall, R. L., and Sharp, H. S. (eds), **Wolf and Man.** Academic Press: New York 1978. 28

45 Harlow, H. F., and Harlow, M. K., 'The Affectional Systems', pp. 287ff. in A. M. Schrier, H. F. Harlow and F. Stolnitz (eds), **Behavior of Non-Human Primates,** vol. II. Academic Press: New York and London 1965. 43, 80

46 Hebb, D. O., 'Emotion in Man and Animal', **Psychological Review** 53.1946 pp. 88ff. 11

47 Hebb, D. O., **The Organization of Behavior.** Wiley: New York 1949. 9, 33

48 Hebb, D. O., and Thompson, W. R., 'The Social Significance of Animal Studies', pp. 329ff. in G. Lindzey and E. Aronson (eds), **Handbook of Social Psychology,** vol II. Addison-Wesley: Reading, Massachusetts 1968. 80

49 Hedeger, H., 'Man as a Social Partner of Animals and Vice Versa', pp. 291ff. in P. E. Ellis (ed.), **Social Organization of Animal Communities.** Academic Press: London 1965. 110

50 Hume, D., **Treatise of Human Nature,** ed. L. A. Selby-Bigge. Oxford: Clarendon Press 1888. 13, 52, 107

51 Jarvis, J. V. M., 'Eusociality in a Mammal: Cooperative Breeding in Naked Mole-Rat Colonies', **Science** 212.1981 p. 571. 56, 99

52 Jenni, D., 'Female Chauvinist Birds', **New Scientist** 82.1979 pp. 896ff. 67

53 Jolly, A., **The Evolution of Primate Behavior.** Mason: New York 1972. 22, 42, 63, 82, 91f., 108

54 Kummer, H., 'Spacing Mechanisms in Social Behavior', pp. 221ff. in Eisenberg and Dillon (1971). 63, 89

55 Kummer, H., 'Aspects of Morality among Non-Human Primates', pp. 35ff. in Stent (1978). 35f., 49

56 Lancaster, J. B., **Primate Behavior and the Emergence of Human Culture.** Holt, Rinehart and Winston: New York 1975. 26, 75, 93

57 Lavery, J. B., and Foley, P. J., 'Altruism or Arousal in the Rat?', **Science** 140.1963 pp. 172f.: repr. pp. 252ff. in Zajonc (1969). 59

58 Lawick-Goodall, J. von, **In the Shadow of Man.** London: Collins 1971. 31, 60, 98

59 Leopold, A., **A Sand County Almanac.** Oxford University Press: New York 1966. 2

60 Leyhausen, P., 'Dominance and Territoriality in Mammalian Social Structure', pp. 22ff. in A. Esser (ed.), **The Uses of Space by Animals and Men.** Plenum: New York 1971. 50, 94

61 Lindauer, M., **Communication among Social Bees.** Harvard: Cambridge, Mass. 1971. 28

62 Linden, E., **Apes, Men and Language.** Dutton: New York 1975. 25, 46, 110

63 Lorenz, K., **King Solomon's Ring,** tr. M. K. Wilson. Methuen: London 1952. 67

64 Lorenz, K., **On Aggression,** tr. M. Latzke. Methuen: London 1966. 5f., 34f., 61, 96

65 Lorenz, K., and Leyhausen, P., **Motivation of Human and Animal Behavior.** Van Nostrand Reinhold: New York 1973. 30, 37, 71, 83, 95

66 McBride, G., 'The Nature-Nurture Problem in Social Evolution', pp. 37ff. in Eisenberg and Dillon (1971). 37, 89

67 McCall, G. J., 'The Social Looking Glass', pp. 274ff. in T. Mischel (ed.), **The Self.** Blackwell: Oxford 1977. 53

68 Mackie, J. L., **Ethics: Inventing Right and Wrong.** Penguin: Harmondsworth 1977. 101

69 Mackie, J. L., 'The Law of the Jungle: Moral Alternatives and Principles of Evolution', **Philosophy** 53.1978 pp. 455ff. 117

70 Matthews, G., 'Animals and the Unity of Psychology', **Philosophy** 53.1978 pp. 437ff. 11

71 Midgley, M., **Beast and Man: The Roots of Human Nature.** Harvester: Hassocks 1979. 13, 41, 58, 107

72 Midgley, M., and Clark, S. R. L., 'The Absence of a Gap between Facts and Values', **Proceedings of the Aristotelian Society** suppl. vol. 54.1980 pp. 207ff. 101, 113, 117

73 Moffat, C. B., 'The Spring Rivalry of Birds', **Irish Naturalist** 12.1903 pp. 152ff.: repr. in Stokes (1974). 68

74 Needham, R., **Belief, Language and Experience.** Blackwell: Oxford 1972. 26

75 Purton, A. C., 'Ethological Categories of Behaviour and Some Consequences of their Behaviour', **Animal Behaviour** 26.1978. pp. 653ff. 10, 56

76 Redican, W. K., 'Adult-Male Infant Interaction in Non-Human Primates', pp. 341ff. in M. E. Lamb (ed.), **The Role of the Father in Child Development.** Wiley: New York 1976. 53, 80

77 Reed, E., **Woman's Evolution.** Pathfinder: New York 1975. 73, 98, 111f.

78 Reed, E., **Sexism and Science.** Pathfinder: New York 1978. 85

79 Reynolds, V., **The Apes.** Cassell: London 1967. 51

80 Reynolds, V., 'Open Groups in Human Evolution', **Man** 1.1966 pp. 441ff. 49, 87

81 Reynolds, V., **The Biology of Human Action.** Freeman: San Francisco 1976. 45

82 Rosenfield, L. C., **From Beast-Machine to Man-Machine.** Octagon Books: New York 1968.

83 Sahlins, M., **Stone Age Economics.** Tavistock: London 1974. 52

84 Sahlins, M., **The Use and Abuse of Biology.** University of Michigan Press: Ann Arbor 1976. 69, 85

85 Savage-Rumbaugh, S., 'The Linguistic Essential', **Science** 210.1980. pp. 922ff. 33

86 Schiller, C. H. (ed.), **Instinctive Behavior.** International Universities Press: New York 1957. 16

87 Sebeok, T. A., and Umiker-Sebeok, J. (eds), **Speaking of Apes.** Plenum: New York and London 1980. 24, 46

88 Seyfarth, R., 'Vervet Monkey Alarm Calls: Semantic Communication in a Free-ranging Primate', **Animal Behaviour** 28.1980 pp. 1070ff. 28

89 Sheldrick, D., **The Tsavo Story.** Collins: London 1973. 89

90 Stent, G. S. (ed.), **Morality as a Biological Phenomenon.** Berlin: Dahlem/Abakon 1978. 23, 35, 49, 53, 106

91 Stokes, A. W. (ed.), **Territory.** Dowden, Hutchinson and Ross: Stroudsberg 1974. 50, 68

92 Temerlin, M. K., **Lucy: Growing Up Human.** Science and Behavior Books: Palo Alto 1975. 45, 73

93 Terrace, H. S., **Nim.** Knopf: New York 1979. 46

94 Tiger, L., and Fox, R., **The Imperial Animal.** Secker and Warburg: London 1971. 84

95 Tinbergen, N., **The Study of Instinct.** Clarendon Press: Oxford 1951. 9, 94

96   Tinbergen, N., 'On War and Peace in Animals and Man', **Science** 160.1968 pp. 1411ff.   64, 88

97   Trivers, R. L., 'The Evolution of Reciprocal Altruism', **Quarterly Review of Biology** 46.1971 pp. 35ff.   51, 57, 85

98   Trivers, R. L., 'Parent-Offspring Conflict', **American Zoologist** 14.1974 pp. 249ff.   86

99   Turnbull, C. M., **The Mountain People.** Cape: London 1973.   13

100 Virgo, H. B., and Waterhouse, M. J., 'The Emergence of Attention Structure among Rhesus Macaques', **Man** 4.1969 pp. 85ff.   92

101 Williams, L., **Man and Monkey.** André Deutsch: London 1967.   92

102 Williams, L., **Challenge to Survival.** Harper & Row: New York 1977.   30, 34, 93, 112

103 Wilson, E. O., 'Competitive and Aggressive Behavior', pp. 183ff. in Eisenberg and Dillon (1971).   83, 89, 90

104 Wilson, E. O., **Sociobiology: The New Synthesis.** Harvard University Press: Cambridge, Mass. 1975.   5, 16, 56, 81, 98f.

105 Wilson, E. O., **On Human Nature.** Harvard University Press: Cambridge, Mass. 1978.   98, 116

106 Wilson, P. J., 'The Promising Primate', **Man** 10.1975 pp. 5ff.   65, 108

107 Zajonc, R. B. (ed.), **Animal Social Psychology.** Wiley: New York 1969.   59

INDEX

abstraction, 31ff., 95ff.

agonistic behaviour, 90 and see hedonic behaviour

aggression, v, 5, 34, 81ff., 88f.

alliance, see lineage

altruism, v, 55ff., 64, 91, 87, 98, 115, 117

ambivalence, 33, 35, 70, 72, 111

Ameslan, 25, 31ff., 45f., 51, 110

amniota, 29, 45, 56

anarchism, 96, 114f.

anthropology, 6, 73f., 83ff.

ants, 28, 55f., 99, 110f.

appeasement, 6, 30, 36, 63, 82 and see presentation

Aristotelianism, 8, 18, 25, 93, 113f.

atomism, 12

aunts, 56, 77, 79ff.

awakening, 1, 44, 47, 53f., 59, 100f., 107, 118

babies, 10, 24, 26, 32, 41ff., 81f., 93

baboons, 34, 63, 66, 71, 74, 75f., 80ff., 84f., 111 and see hamadryas

baby-battering, 81f., 85f.

Bacon, Francis, 9, 21

badgers, 96

bees, 28ff.

behaviourism, 13f.

belief, 22f., 36

bestiaries, v, 7, 98

biograms, 88

birds, 19, 50, 64, 67f., 74, 83, 89, 93

brain damage, 23, 32

butterflies, 7, 50

cats, 19, 30, 41, 48, 74, 83

captivity, 37f. and see domestication

cause, 9, 41, 101ff.

chaffinch, 19

chance, 11, 69

chastity, 76, 85

Chesterton, G. K., 1

children, 32, 35, 37, 41f., 79ff., 91

chimpanzees, 7, 9, 22, 25ff., 29ff., 33f., 36, 45f., 49, 60f., 65, 72, 74, 82, 88, 92, 110f.

claims, 50, 96f.

Clever Hans, 24

cognitive maps, 28, 48, 60

cohort, 74f., 80, 83f.

communication, 14, 26ff., 35

conscience, 34ff., 42ff., 101ff. and see shame

consciousness, 14, 18 and see subjectivity

contractarianism, 101f., 114

cuckoos, 65, 79, 94

culture, 68ff. and see anthropology

cuteness, 32, 81

dance flies, 35

Dante Alighieri, 23

Darwin, Charles R., 67f.

death, 44, 53f., 59, 61

deer, red, 75

Descartes, Rene, 14, 17, 24, 45

desire, 22f., 35

determinism, 38ff.

dogs, 2, 13, 23f., 61

domestication, 110f.

dominance, 6, 30, 36, 38, 75ff., 82f., 88ff.

doves, 34

duty, 40, 94f., 100ff.

Ecclesiastes, 114

egoism, 55ff., 60 and see altruism, self-awareness

elephants, 24, 53, 67, 80, 89

emotion, 23f.

empathy, 1, 11, 15, 43, 111

epistemology, 1f., 14, 17, 21, 39f., 44, 101f.

ethical, 107

evolutionary ethics, 61, 99ff.

evolutionary theory, 11, 55ff., 64f., 68f., 72ff., 79f., 85f., 91, 99f., 112

fetishism, 72

fish, 64, 83, 88f., 99

final causes, 9f., 103f.

flatworms, 27

forethought, 16, 23, 47, 51, 55f., 60, 70, 93, 95, 113

fowls, 91

freedom, 37f., 71f., 96, 115

function, 10, 64, 79, 80f., 99f. and see goal

Index

Index

127

MORE OXFORD PAPERBACKS

Details of other Oxford Paperbacks are given on following pages. A complete list, including books in the World's Classics, Past Masters and OPUS Series, can be obtained from the General Publicity Department, Oxford University Press, Walton Street, Oxford OX2 6DP.

THE EXPANDING CIRCLE
Ethics and Sociobiology
Peter Singer

Where do ethical standards come from? Are our notions of good and evil created by reason, or by evolution? Can society shape its own destiny, or must it merely reflect biological imperatives? In answering these questions Peter Singer (author of the widely acclaimed *Animal Liberation*) is particularly concerned with the light thrown on our morality by the new science of sociobiology. He builds up a convincing picture of an ethical system which, though biologically grounded, has expanded from this base to become more rational and objective.

'Unwaveringly clear, rigorously accessible' *Sunday Times*

MEN AND WOMEN
How different are they?
John Nicholson

Dr Nicholson considers that it is high time that some of our civilization's many myths about the differences between the attitude and behaviour of the two sexes were quashed. In this revised and expanded edition of his popular and successful book, *A Question of Sex*, he brings us more startling conclusions about the real similarities and differences between the sexes.

MORAL PHILOSOPHY
D. D. Raphael

Unlike most 'introductions' to moral philosophy, which in fact presuppose a fair acquaintance with the subject, this book is written expressly as a genuine introduction for the beginner. It is not confined to the theory of ethics in any narrow sense, but demonstrates the connections between abstract ethics and practical problems in law and government, and in the social sciences generally.

'It would be difficult to find a clearer introduction to modern moral philosophy.' *Tablet*

OPUS

AN INTRODUCTION TO THE STUDY OF MAN
J. Z. Young

There are many ways of approaching the study of Man. Professor Young believes that biological knowledge provides a useful framework to help us to understand ourselves. Modern biology embraces many disciplines, and in this book a synthesis is made tracing the sources of human activity from their biochemical basis to the highest levels of consciousness.

'Professor Young sticks to straight and informative science ... is rivetingly interesting, and conveys a constant sense of the controlled, critical curiosity which is what science is about' *Guardian*

'an impressive performance' *Observer*

ETHICS SINCE 1900
Third Edition
Mary Warnock

Mary Warnock's well-informed and discriminating account explores the main ethical problems which have been discussed in the present century in England, the United States, and France. Among others, the writings of Moore, Prichard, Ayer, Stevenson, Hare, Sartre, and Rawls are discussed and analysed in detail.

'In this lively and fascinating book Mrs Warnock tells with admirable clarity the story of the development of English moral philosophy in the twentieth century . . . most attractively written, spontaneous, forthright and unfuzzy.' *Times Literary Supplement*

OPUS

DARWIN
Jonathan Howard

Darwin's theory that men's ancestors were apes caused a
furore in the scientific world and outside it when *The Origin of
Species* was published in 1859. Arguments still rage about the
implications of his evolutionary theory, and scepticism about
the value of Darwin's contribution to knowledge is widespread.
In this analysis of Darwin's major insights and arguments,
Jonathan Howard reasserts the importance of Darwin's work
for the development of modern biology.

'Jonathan Howard has produced an intellectual *tour de force*, a
classic in the genre of popular scientific exposition which will
still be read in fifty years' time.'   *Times Literary Supplement*

Past Masters

THE NATURE OF HUMAN AGGRESSION
Ashley Montagu

Is man a born killer? In one of the most important books of his career, Ashley Montagu debunks this currently fashionable theory. He takes issue with the innate aggressionists – Konrad Lorenz, Robert Ardrey, Niko Tinbergen, Desmond Morris and others – and shows that 'on every one of the fundamental claims they have made concerning man's allegedly instinctive aggressive drives, they are demonstrably wrong'.

'a vigorous book attacking the nonsense . . . concerning the inherent aggressiveness of Man. It should not still need writing.' *Guardian*

'a counsel of hope rather than one of despair – and one based on a realistic, cogently-argued view of man's nature' *Times Educational Supplement*